SAUCES
FRENCH
AND
FAMOUS

SAUCES
FRENCH
AND
FAMOUS

❧

by
Louis Diat

DOVER PUBLICATIONS, INC.
NEW YORK

Published in Canada by General Publishing
Company, Ltd., 30 Lesmill Road, Don Mills,
Toronto, Ontario.
Published in the United Kingdom by Constable
and Company, Ltd., 10 Orange Street, London
WC2H 7EG.

This Dover edition, first published in 1978, is
an unabridged republication of the work as published by Rinehart & Co., New York, in 1951.

International Standard Book Number:
0-486-23663-3
Library of Congress Catalog Card Number:
78-51528

Manufactured in the United States of America
Dover Publications, Inc.
180 Varick Street
New York, N.Y. 10014

CONTENTS

CONTENTS

FOREWORD

WHEN Louis Diat asked me to write the foreword to this book, I was very flattered, just as I was when he asked me some ten years ago to edit the manuscript of his first one. During these years we have worked together on three books—including this one—and on many magazine articles. His were the recipes, of course; and his the know-how of French cookery, naturelle-ment. My contribution was phrasing his knowledge in cookery English which American housewives can easily comprehend and put into practice. To do this I have watched the renowned Ritz cuisine brought to perfection under his guidance in the kitchens of the erstwhile New York Ritz Carlton Hotel, I have been taught French cooking in my own kitchen while playing a fumbling role of apprenti *under the direction of this great culinary master, and I have worked many profitable hours at the desk with him, writing and correcting recipes and learning the lore of the French cuisine. Mine has, indeed, been a rare and enviable privilege.*

After these ten years I feel I can say with the utmost confidence that Louis Diat knows fine French cooking probably better than any person living today. Apprenticed at the turn of the century before our modern, simpler eating habits replaced the culinary triumphs of France, his background has enabled him to put the essence of those famous and wonderful dishes into the less complicated ones now preferred. This skill is, I believe, one secret of the Ritz

7

cuisine which has been his singular contribution to American gastronomy.

When Louis Diat writes of French cooking it is never as an outsider looking in—not, for example, as a traveler to France obtaining a recipe from this little bistro today, that great hostelry tomorrow and a well-publicized provincial auberge next week. Nor does he write from the viewpoint of one whose quickly acquired knowledge grew out of an adult eagerness to write about French cookery. No, his has been a lifetime of French cooking that started with a childhood French home where even simple cooking was an art, progressed to an early and thorough training in the chef's trade, and then was perfected under the most exacting masters in the continent's greatest hotels. He writes from the inside looking out, and he does it because of the endless requests made upon him for recipes and cookery guidance.

Mr. Diat has, as I have said, the unique ability of being able to turn the complicated formulas of the French haute cuisine *into equally satisfying but simple recipes which any earnest novice can follow. This book is a perfect example of that. But he is also able to evolve extraordinary dishes out of some of the simple recipes of the French countryside, and the following story of the evolution of the well-known Vichyssoise shows this phase of his art.*

When the Ritz Carlton opened its roof-garden restaurant, Chef Diat added to his menus many new dishes especially appropriate for summer dining in hot New York. Searching for a "different" soup, he recalled the potato-and-leek potage of his home in France and how his mother solved the problem of her children's resistance to hot soup in summer by cooling it for them with cold, rich milk. Diat took this idea but for his sophisticated clientele refined the soup by straining it several times, adding plenty of cream and chilling it thoroughly. The result was a luscious soup, satiny smooth and very cold, which he sprinkled with chopped chives for a bright garnish and added flavor. The name honored the housewives of Vichy, then a famous watering place near his boyhood home. Although it probably does not belong in a book devoted to sauces, I am including the original recipe in this foreword because it is one recipe that every person wants from Louis Diat.

To make Vichyssoise: Clean and chop the white parts of 4 leeks or enough to make 1½ cups and combine with ½ cup chopped onion. Melt 1 tablespoon butter in a saucepan, add leeks and onion and cook gently until they are soft but not brown. Add 1 quart boiling water and 5 medium potatoes, peeled and chopped, and 1 tablespoon salt. Cook until potatoes are well done, about 30 minutes. Strain through a fine sieve or food mill. Return the purée to the pan, add 2 cups each of milk and medium cream. Bring back to the boil and then strain through a very fine sieve. Cool, stirring occasionally. When cold strain again and add 1 cup heavy cream. Mix well and chill before serving. For a bright garnish and more flavor sprinkle with chopped chives. This makes 9 to 10 cups.

Gourmets seem to agree that the most neglected phase of American cookery is in the realm of sauces. I am sure that they will find in this book by Louis Diat the long needed guide to the art of sauce making by which a more distinguished cuisine can be achieved.

HELEN E. RIDLEY

New York City

PREFACE

TO cook like a French chef seems to be a goal of more and more English-speaking people, and that includes men who have taken up cooking as a hobby as well as women who want to give their families and guests a distinguished cuisine. But when I call to mind the questions that come to me from these culinary neophytes, many of whom have become extremely skilful in other of the cookery arts, I realize that making fine sauces is something they have not mastered. Yet who ever heard of a good French chef who was not first a good saucier? Thus a nagging urgency to do a complete book on French sauces and their place in fine meals has dogged my mind for some time. It seemed the logical book to follow the two previous ones I have written on French cooking.

A great deal of thought has gone into this book because of my desire to help people to a better understanding of sauce cookery, an understanding which tells when to add the sauce that best complements the fine cut of meat or species of fish and creates an elegance that otherwise would be missing, or which guides the selection of the sauce for an inexpensive food and brings forth a really distinguished dish from something that in itself is mediocre. A major aim has been to clarify and simplify the making of all the important French sauces and of most of the less familiar ones, too. I have tried sincerely to explain every detail carefully, have given quantities suitable for *family meals serving five or six and home entertaining, and have kept in mind the utensils found in home kitchens. If only two or three servings are required most of the recipes can be cut in half.*

The housewife or her cuisinière *in any French home, be it haut* monde or paysanne, *city or farm home, can easily and consistently serve magnificent meals from simple ingredients and with few utensils because she gets the most out of what she has. Not least in her skill is an ability to turn out exquisite sauces. In this she is never backward in making the chef's secrets a part of her repertoire. With this book as a guide, I trust my readers will make my knowledge of sauces a part of theirs.*

L. D.

INTRODUCTION

LOVERS of fine food call French sauces the gift that French cooking has given the world. They believe, in fact, that *la cuisine française* and *les sauces françaises* are the inseparable twins of French culinary art. And this belief is certainly confirmed by literature, since the one seldom exists without the other. It is no exaggeration to say that it is very difficult to try to count up the number of sauces generally popular and regularly served in France. And how seriously the French take their sauces is further evidenced by the generations of proud Frenchmen who have boasted that no matter where you might go in France, whether to a simple farmer's cottage or an expensive Parisian restaurant, you will always find cooking brought to a high peak of excellence by means of the most mouth-watering sauces.

So, skill in French cooking, either professional or amateur, means knowing the sauces and being able to make them expertly. For a gourmet a mere familiarity with the different sauces is hardly enough. He must roll the flavourful mixtures over his tongue savouring all the nuances – and develops a high gastronomic fever if perfection is missed. Otherwise half the pleasure of eating a sauce would be lost. And for the one who loves to cook, there is hardly a greater satisfaction than putting together the combinations that produce sauces which are topics of conversation, sauces lovingly and tirelessly blended and cooked for perfect flavour and texture.

In my training to be a chef, the work with sauces was the most important part of a long and arduous apprenticeship. I look back upon the fourteen-hour days – sometimes longer – at the Maison Calondre in Moulins, where I first learned how professionals make sauces and how they use them. I recall only too clearly my days in the great kitchens of the Paris Ritz, where I had the opportunity of perfecting my skill under its famous *saucier*. I can see myself, a very young *sous chef*, in front of a hot range pushing and turning a sturdy wooden spatula as the sauces reduced in the big copper pans, and standing with bated breath while the *chef des cuisines* went through his daily routine of tasting the sauces for the day. The practised eye and sensitive tongue of this culinary expert could detect the slightest deviation from perfection and his Gallic temper soon let the kitchen know it. *Zut!* Down the sink drain would go what we had thought a perfectly good sauce, and to the tune of a torrent of French fury. The *saucier* would yell for fresh butter, cream, stock, egg yolks or whatever was needed. Then all over again the big wooden spatula would be pushed back and forth and around, back and forth and around in the big copper pan. And more often than not the hand trembled a bit, because it was no secret that too many mishaps could suddenly cut short one's ambition to rise to be a great *saucier* and following that, on to the final pinnacle, a *chef des cuisines* in one's own right.

Fortunately in home cooking the skill of sauce making can be learned in less arduous ways, and families, *grace à Dieu*, are usually not quite so exacting as *les chefs des cuisines*. At the same time, many eager cooks find it difficult to achieve our results in their home kitchens. The quantities we handle, the utensils we use and the ways we work are all so different from cooking *en famille*. This is one reason, and a major one, why you are so often puzzled in trying to follow recipes secured from professional chefs. It isn't that a chef doesn't want to give you his recipes and his cookery techniques – what some people feel are his secrets. And sometimes there is also a language handicap, the difficulty that anyone experiences in trying to explain in any but his native tongue the trade he has learned and the skill acquired in practising it. But more important is the fact that it is almost impossible to describe French sauces merely through recipes. The principles and techniques involved in making sauces the French way, the hows and whys of the roux, the reduction, the finishing and so on, should first be clearly understood. With the French, sauce making is an art and whoever wishes to achieve his success must approach the subject in that spirit.

But anyone who likes to cook can become expert in no time by following the rules. They include such basic ones as using good ingredients, using seasonings with discretion, stirring, straining, swirling the butter into a mixture, or whatever the directions call for, but always doing these things carefully and exactly. Then with enough practice at the range artistic perfection is assured. Once mastered, this ability to make consistently fine sauces is like any other art, a priceless possession that you never lose.

CONVERSION TABLES FOR FOREIGN EQUIVALENTS

DRY INGREDIENTS

Ounces		Grams	Grams		Ounces	Pounds		Kilograms	Kilograms		Pounds
1	=	28.35	1	=	0.035	1	=	0.454	1	=	2.205
2		56.70	2		0.07	2		0.91	2		4.41
3		85.05	3		0.11	3		1.36	3		6.61
4		113.40	4		0.14	4		1.81	4		8.82
5		141.75	5		0.18	5		2.27	5		11.02
6		170.10	6		0.21	6		2.72	6		13.23
7		198.45	7		0.25	7		3.18	7		15.43
8		226.80	8		0.28	8		3.63	8		17.64
9		255.15	9		0.32	9		4.08	9		19.84
10		283.50	10		0.35	10		4.54	10		22.05
11		311.85	11		0.39	11		4.99	11		24.26
12		340.20	12		0.42	12		5.44	12		26.46
13		368.55	13		0.46	13		5.90	13		28.67
14		396.90	14		0.49	14		6.35	14		30.87
15		425.25	15		0.53	15		6.81	15		33.08
16		453.60	16		0.57						

LIQUID INGREDIENTS

Liquid Ounces		Milliliters	Milliliters		Liquid Ounces	Quarts		Liters	Liters		Quarts
1	=	29.573	1	=	0.034	1	=	0.946	1	=	1.057
2		59.15	2		0.07	2		1.89	2		2.11
3		88.72	3		0.10	3		2.84	3		3.17
4		118.30	4		0.14	4		3.79	4		4.23
5		147.87	5		0.17	5		4.73	5		5.28
6		177.44	6		0.20	6		5.68	6		6.34
7		207.02	7		0.24	7		6.62	7		7.40
8		236.59	8		0.27	8		7.57	8		8.45
9		266.16	9		0.30	9		8.52	9		9.51
10		295.73	10		0.33	10		9.47	10		10.57

Gallons (American)		Liters	Liters		Gallons (American)
1	=	3.785	1	=	0.264
2		7.57	2		0.53
3		11.36	3		0.79
4		15.14	4		1.06
5		18.93	5		1.32
6		22.71	6		1.59
7		26.50	7		1.85
8		30.28	8		2.11
9		34.07	9		2.38
10		37.86	10		2.74

SAUCES
FRENCH
AND
FAMOUS

I. SAUCES THE FRENCH WAY

I. SAUCES THE FRENCH WAY

MOST important utensil in a French kitchen is the saucepan. Out of its copper depths generations of French cooks have brought forth the succulent dishes that have made their cookery so famous. And out of it, I am sure, they will continue to bring forth those dishes for generations to come. Put a French woman in a kitchen with a copper saucepan – and a clay marmite, of course – give her only the simplest ingredients and she will turn out a meal whose deliciousness lingers for ever in the memory. Put the same saucepan – and marmite – in the hands of a French chef and such a succession of magnificent feasts come forth that you wonder from whence the magic springs.

But fortunately there is no special alchemy associated with the French saucepan. It hides no secrets understood only by the native sons. You, too, can coax the same French specialties out of a saucepan. Your praises, too, will be sung by all who eat your cooking. That is, if you appreciate fine food yourself, if you have an eagerness to learn how to prepare it and if you are willing to perfect the art with practice. You can, however, be helped in achieving your aims if you understand the principles on which French sauced cookery is based, the relationship between the foodstuffs in the meal and their enhancing sauces. Recipes then will merely serve to point the way to exciting new ventures along a well-known and well-loved route.

In French cooking the word sauce means any liquid or semi-liquid adjunct that complements a dish. It includes, of course, the gravy on the stew and the cream sauce on the cauliflower. But it also encompasses salad dressings, melted-butter dressings and other appetite-provoking additions. In French cooking a sauce is always chosen with an eye to complementing the robustness or delicacy or other characteristic of a food. For example, a Mornay Sauce with all its delectability would not be served on a vegetable or a fish if a simple butter-and-lemon dressing were more suitable. And a good French cook would not put cheese in every Cream Sauce just because cheese is often desirable. This meticulous attention to flavours and their complements is also applied to food textures. Compare the smooth satiny Hollandaise that does so much for poached salmon and the crunchiness of Polonaise that offsets the smoothness of noodles. And don't make the mistake made by so many people of thinking that French sauces are just always thick and rich. They can be and often are very thin and piquant like Vinaigrette or thin and savoury like a simple shallot and wine sauce for sautéed meat.

It is a fact, however, that the word sauce does imply a thickened liquid and it is also a fact that most sauces are thickened, the thickenings most commonly used being flour and egg yolks. But from what I know of the sauces of many countries, I believe that French sauces are never quite as thick as the others. The standard of thickness of a fine French sauce is termed *du corps,* meaning having a certain 'body' or sometimes it is described as *à la nappe,* meaning an adequate coating. In other words, the sauce may be relatively thin, and very frequently is, but it has a definite recognizable consistency or 'body', and when it sauces a food it can be depended upon to really coat it. It will not be runny or watery. On the other hand, you will seldom see, for example, a French Brown Sauce having the thick pasty consistency that I have seen in so many American brown gravies.

It is a fact, too, that a great many French sauces are rich, but here again the characteristic richness has a difference. Richness does not mean fattiness. Except in the case of the Hollandaise type of sauces that depend upon butter for their consistency and the cold sauces that employ large proportions of salad oils, French sauces are never loaded with the fat of the meat drippings or even with butter. Nor are fatty cheeses ever used. Richness comes from such ingredients as cream, egg yolks, and the concentration of wine and stock; butter is used as a carrier for the flour and to impart a characteristic flavour and texture; and cheese is to give a subtle flavour without changing the texture of the sauce, hence the dry types are always used.

WHAT GOES INTO SAUCES

The liquid ingredient, obviously very important, should always be selected for its suitability. It may be milk, cream, wine, stock, tomato juice or other flavourful liquid. Or marinade used for game or meat, or the juice that cooks out of meat. Most often it is a combination of several of these ingredients and very frequently it is the water in which meat or poultry is cooked, as in the case of stews and fricassees. Delicate and light-coloured foods are usually sauced with the lighter sauces made with milk, cream or white wine, while darker meats such as beef and game are more often complemented by a darker sauce. But this is far from being a hard and fast rule. The contrast of a light sauce with a dark meat or a brown sauce with a light one makes many dishes more interesting. For example, the delicate Cream Sauces for furred and feathered game, the Tomato Sauces for chicken and the browned Butter Sauces for fish.

In using the liquids in White and Brown Sauces the French add a greater proportion of liquid than Americans or English do and then the sauce is cooked down or in the language of the kitchen 'reduced' to the desired consistency. This reduction is extremely important because it develops a more velvety and delicate texture and gives each ingredient in the saucepan an opportunity to release its best flavour. The finished sauce has a well-blended savour only obtainable in a mixture that has been slowly concentrated or 'reduced'.

Regardless of what liquid is used, a sauce will always be improved if it is possible to include in it some of the flavour of the food. Using all or a portion of the water in which fish was poached or the marinade of meat or game, the juice in the roasting pan and the brown crustiness left in the pan where meat was sautéed are ways of carrying the flavour of a food into its sauce. In many instances the sauce is made right in the pan in which the food was cooked. A Frenchman is shocked no end at seeing a sauce made in a separate pan and poured over a food while all the flavour of the juices is discarded from the cooking pan. The recipes at the end of the White, Brown and Game Sauce chapters include examples of making a sauce in the pan in which the food was cooked.

It is best to use the liquids called for in the recipe but when they are not available substitutions often can be made. For example, water with a little lemon juice or water in which mushrooms have been cooked can be substituted for wine. When white stock is not on hand, water or water in which mushrooms have been cooked can again be used. For brown stock, substitute water and tomato juice. Or use a bouillon cube dissolved in water. Since stock can be made from bones (page 30) and it will keep for some time in the refrigerator, it is both practical and inexpensive to have some on hand. Water can be used instead of fish stock, but in cooking fish fillets, added flavour is obtained by laying the bones that have been removed on top of the fish.

The kind of wine to use is puzzling to some people. The first requisite is that it be a dry wine and the second that it be a good one. A good wine sauce can never be made from a poor wine. It doesn't have to be a vintage wine, however, and it can be an inexpensive one. But it can't be a wine that you wouldn't want to drink from a glass. How good it is depends upon how it is to be used. If it is to be reduced to almost nothing in the pan with shallots it can be a less expensive wine, if the recipe calls for reduction by half it should be a better one and if it is to be added at the end of cooking just before serving the sauce, as Sherry and Madeira are often used, it should be a very good wine.

Most sauces contain some fat or, in the case of cold sauces, oil. Fat adds flavour, it serves to blend in the flour when that is used and it produces a characteristic thickness particularly in the Hollandaise types of sauces. But no other fat can be compared with butter. In delicate White Sauces its fine flavour is a requisite, and in the more robust Brown Sauces the finish with butter adds a flavour and texture obtained in no other way. Finally there are the Butter Sauces themselves, which consist entirely of butter flavoured with tarragon, lobster, lemon and so on.

In France butter is unusually good because most cities are quite closely surrounded by fertile farming sections and the freshly made butter arrives daily. It is often unsalted, purchased in small amounts and used quickly. And what sauces it makes! But the French consider butter in a slightly different light than other nations. They are not at all concerned with the need for butter to eat on breadstuffs. In fact, they seldom spread it on those thick slices of light, crusty bread they like so well or on their rolls, croissants and brioches. Of course they always break off small pieces of the bread to mop up from the plate the last vestiges of a good sauce. That is *vraiment le bon goût* - really good eating. Their butter is in the sauce and nothing can take its place.

For actual cooking of meat or fish, that is, when sautéed or roasted, it is not necessary to use butter. It is a needless extravagance and it is apt to burn when subjected to high heat. Use good suet, fresh pork fat, fresh sweet drippings or a good salad oil for frying or for basting a roast. But when you come to making the sauce - or gravy - never use the cooking fat. Discard it all from the pan and (without washing the pan) put in butter to make the sauce.

All the many seasonings that go into French sauces are considered very carefully. There are a few general rules that you will do well to remember. Be careful with the salt, because reducing a sauce concentrates it and using stock adds salt, too. You'll find that it is only too easy to oversalt a sauce. Add pepper near the end, because long cooking is apt to develop a slightly bitter taste. When a recipe calls for shallots you can substitute onion, even though the former give a better flavour. Shallots, butter and wine are a combination that blend to make an unusual savouriness which I know no other way of achieving. When a faggot is specified, tuck the parsley, bay leaf and thyme in the curved side of the piece of celery stalk and place another piece of celery on top. Then wind and wind the little bundle with clean white string to hold it firmly together. If sprigs of parsley are cooked in a sauce, lift them out before straining or else be careful not to rub them through the sieve otherwise there will be unattractive dark specks all through the sauce. In preparing mushrooms to add to a sauce, cook them in a little salted water with a few drops of lemon juice and they will not darken. Never throw this liquid away. If you don't use it in the sauce, save it and add to some other sauce you may be making.

HOW SAUCES ARE THICKENED

Of the various ways of thickening sauces, the most common is with a roux. This is a carefully cooked mixture of fat and flour, usually equal amounts, with butter the preferred fat. The roux can be *blanc*, *blond* or *brun*, that is white, golden or brown. The longer the mixture cooks the darker it gets and obviously a white roux is for the whiter sauces, a brown one for dark sauces. A properly cooked roux gets you off to a good start; a poorly cooked one may be the reason why a finished sauce falls short of perfection. You must have sufficient butter to blend the flour and you must cook the mixture over a low heat so that the starch grains can expand, stirring it constantly. Rapid cooking shrivels the starch grains causing a grainy, less smooth sauce. Neglecting to stir results in uneven cooking and in the case of a brown roux produces a spotty browning, often with burned specks, which in turn affects both flavour and texture.

A sauce thickened with a roux is started by melting the butter, adding the flour and cooking the two together. Then the liquid, which should be hot, is added. As cooking continues the mixture must be stirred constantly until it thickens and after that frequently during the slow gentle cooking that reduces it to the proper thickness. These rules insure a smooth sauce with a homogeneous consistency that is free from lumps. There are many times, however, when a sauce is made with the liquid in which a food has been cooked, for example, when fish is poached in wine or when making a stew. Then the sauce must be thickened at the end of cooking. In these instances, French recipes usually direct the use of Béchamel, Velouté or Cream Sauce and sometimes Tomato Sauce to finish and thicken the liquid. Or Manie Butter – *Beurre Manié* – which is butter creamed with flour, can be used. Manie Butter can also replace the Béchamel or other sauce specified in a recipe but which you may not have on hand. For instance if the recipe calls for one fourth to one half cup of Cream Sauce you can add one half cup of cream and then finish with Manie Butter made with one tablespoon butter creamed with one teaspoon of flour. The same proportions can be used to replace Tomato Sauce using, of course, tomato purée or strained canned tomatoes and the Manie Butter. In using Manie Butter you merely stir it into the hot liquid and let it cook only until it is blended in. Do not boil it. This is always a convenient way of bringing a thin sauce up to a desired thickness.

Another thickening agent is egg yolk, usually for sauces made with milk or cream. Actually egg yolks do more than thicken, they add a richness of flavour, an attractive colour, and give a delectable, satiny-smooth quality. But unless carefully added they can also curdle a sauce. Dropping egg yolks into a hot mixture is fatal. They coagulate and ruin your sauce. To combine egg yolks in a hot sauce, first mix them with a little cream. Then stir in some of the hot liquid, and when this is well combined turn it back into the remaining hot sauce in the pan, stirring briskly all the time. The minute it reaches a boil remove from the heat to prevent curdling.

Sauces like Hollandaise, Bearnaise and Mayonnaise are emulsions and their characteristic thickness can only be achieved if the melted butter or the oil is stirred into the egg yolks very gradually. and mixed in very thoroughly. In the case of Hollandaise and Bearnaise it is also necessary to keep the cooking temperature down. Always use a double boiler and each time the water in the bottom pan reaches the boiling point add a spoonful or two of cold water to keep it continually just below boiling.

Good French *sauciers* – that is, sauce chefs – also finish a great many sauces with butter, which adds flavour but which also serves, if correctly combined, to make a very, light delicate sauce just a trifle thicker. To do this add a spoonful of butter to the hot sauce and then move the pan in a circular motion, swirling in the butter. Remove the pan from the heat when the butter has barely melted. The trick is not to stir with a spoon and not to cook the sauce after adding the butter.

STRAINING AND STORING SAUCES

Straining is considered very important, too. Naturally a sauce that contains such ingredients as mushrooms wouldn't be strained, but as a rule the smoother most of the sauces are the better they are, and so they are run through a fine sieve or a muslin cloth. I have not suggested the latter in this recipe book because it is not too practical in home kitchens. But in the hotel most of the basic hot sauces are strained through cloth. Two chefs, one at each end of a great square of muslin, twist it slowly until all the sauce has been gradually squeezed out. Bits of onion or shallot, an occasional small lump of flour, those tiny strings of egg white that cling to the yolk, perhaps a few peppercorns are some of the undesirable bits that are held back. But more important is the fact that the straining of a sauce seems to improve its texture.

Several of the basic sauces, namely Velouté, Tomato Sauce and Brown Sauce, can be stored in the refrigerator for at least a week. But it is not advisable to do this with any that contain milk, cream or eggs. Béchamel will keep for a couple of days but it is hardly safe to keep it any longer. The sauces should be stored in a covered jar and any of the first three named can be reheated at the end of a week, returned to a clean jar and kept another week. Or if a little Sherry is poured over the top of Tomato Sauce or Brown Sauce either one will keep longer without reheating. Pouring a little melted fat over them and also over Velouté to seal the top is another way to hold longer, using, of course, a nice sweet fresh fat.

FOUNDATION INGREDIENTS

To become skilled in making sauced dishes the French way you need to know how to make the foundation stocks and marinades which give so many of the recipes their characteristic flavour. Stock can be made up occasionally and stored in the refrigerator in a covered jar and kept for a long time if it is boiled up and returned to a clean jar every week or ten days. If, however, this is not practical a canned consommé can be used or bouillon cubes dissolved in water.

The following recipes are for the ingredient stocks and marinades. The recipe for Rouennaise is given because it is usually spread on the toast used to garnish game dishes, and although not actually a sauce it is an important adjunct.

BROWN STOCK

1 to 2 pounds beef bones
1 to 2 pounds veal bones
1 sliced carrot
½ tablespoon salt
2 sliced onions

2½ quarts water
A faggot made by tying together 2 stalks celery, 4 sprigs parsley, a little thyme and a small bay leaf

Spread bones in a shallow roasting pan, strew carrot and onions over and place in a moderately hot oven of 400 degrees and let cook until they are a very rich dark brown. Transfer to soup kettle, add water, salt and faggot and bring slowly to the boil, skimming when necessary. Continue cooking slowly for 4 hours, when water should be reduced to about 2 quarts. Strain through a fine sieve or cheesecloth. Store in refrigerator until needed for making sauces which call for Brown Stock and for Brown Sauce. This stock can also be used to make French Onion Soup or vegetable soup.

WHITE STOCK

1 pound veal or chicken bones (or both)
2½ quarts cold water
1 teaspoon salt
1 carrot

2 onions
2 leeks
A faggot made by tying together 3 sprigs parsley, 1 stalk celery, a little thyme and a small bay leaf

Cover the bones with water and parboil for a few minutes just long enough to bring the first scum to rise to the top. Skim, drain and cover with the 2½ quarts fresh cold water. Add remaining ingredients, bring to a boil and simmer very slowly for about 3 hours. Remove fat, strain and store in refrigerator until needed. Do not keep longer than a week. This makes 3 pints of stock. It is used as the liquid for Velouté and in many White Sauces.

FISH STOCK

Fish bones and head (Dover
   sole or salmon preferred)
1½ quarts water
½ teaspoon salt
1 onion

1 carrot
A faggot made by tying together
   1 stalk celery, 3 sprigs
   parsley, a little thyme and
   a bay leaf

Cook all together for about 20 minutes. Strain. This makes about 1 quart of stock. Used for the liquid for Fish Velouté and in many fish sauces.

MEAT GRAVY

This is not the flour-thickened type of gravy that is familiar to many. By meat gravy, I mean the juice and drippings of the roast meat that have browned in the roasting pan, diluted with water and reduced to concentrate the flavour. To get a rich-flavoured gravy the meat should be salted and spread with fat – either beef, veal or pork (butter gives a more delicate flavour to chicken gravy) – when put in the roasting pan, and a few slices of onion and carrot are put in the roasting pan, too. Baste the meat with the fat during roasting and if there seems to be any chance of the fat and drippings scorching, add a very little water to the pan. When the meat is done, remove from the pan and discard all the fat. Add water to the pan and cook on top of the range, stirring in all the brown crustiness that has formed on the bottom and around the edges of the pan. Then, when the meat is carved, add any juice that escapes on the dish. This gravy is served with the meat, of course, but whatever is left should be kept in the refrigerator to add to any Brown Sauces you may be making.

MUSHROOM DUXELLES

¼ pound mushrooms   ½ teaspoon salt
2 tablespoons butter   1 teaspoon chopped parsley
1 teaspoon chopped shallot (or onion)

Clean mushrooms, dry thoroughly and chop very fine. Melt butter, add shallot (or onion) and mushrooms. Cook until all the moisture is cooked away and add salt and parsley. Use as directed in recipes.

UNCOOKED MARINADE

2 thinly sliced onions   A little thyme
1 thinly sliced carrot   2 bay leaves
2 minced shallots (if available) 12 peppercorns
1 clove of garlic   2 cloves
2 stalks celery   2 cups red or white wine
1 teaspoon salt   ½ cup salad oil

Mix together all ingredients and pour over meat to be marinated.

COOKED MARINADE

1 quart water   1 chopped carrot   4 sprigs parsley
1½ cups vinegar   1 clove garlic   12 peppercorns
2 chopped onions 1 teaspoon thyme   1 tablespoon salt

Put all ingredients in a saucepan, bring to a boil and cook gently for 1 hour. Cool and pour over meat to be marinated.

ROUENNAISE

2 tablespoons salt-pork fat
1 cup duck or chicken livers
A little thyme
1 bay leaf

1 teaspoon salt
A little pepper
1 pony (2 ounces) Cognac or dry
Sherry

Melt fat and heat until it is very, very hot. Add livers, thyme, bay leaf, salt and pepper and cook 3 to 4 minutes over a hot fire. Add Cognac or Sherry and mix all together, crushing the livers in mixing. Rub through a fine sieve to make a paste. Used for spreading on the toast on which game is served. May also be used as a spread for canapés.

II. WHITE SAUCES

II. WHITE SAUCES

THE White Sauces are light in colour as their name implies, usually a creamy white or white tinged with the yellow that egg yolks give. Perfection is recognized by a delicate, satiny smoothness which is achieved only when the flour is slowly cooked in the butter and the liquid carefully reduced to the right consistency. It is also recognized by a complete blending of the ingredients which produces a well-defined flavour that is never heavy or harsh.

The sauces in this group are evolved from two basic ones, Béchamel and Velouté, and their four major variations Cream, Mornay, Suprême and Allemande. Or they follow the general technique of making White Sauces but with some other liquid substituted for the milk or stock, such as the use of wine and water in making a fish sauce. Or one of the basic group like Velouté or Cream Sauce is used instead of a roux as the thickening, as in making Curry Sauce.

Béchamel, made with butter, flour and milk is served 'as is' on many foods and is also the foundation upon which Cream Sauce – *Sauce Crème* – and Mornay Sauce are made. In making Cream Sauce heavy cream is added to Béchamel, while Mornay Sauce is Béchamel further thickened with cream and egg yolks and flavoured with cheese. Velouté, made with butter, flour and white stock, is the foundation for Suprême Sauce and Allemande. For Suprême Sauce the Velouté is combined with mushroom liquor, then reduced and finally enriched with heavy cream; and in making Allemande, the Suprême Sauce is thickened further with egg yolks and made still richer with more cream. Large hotel kitchens keep these six sauces always on hand ready for the dishes that require them. Scores of different sauces are also made by combining these in varying amounts with other ingredients, and it is usually possible to use either Béchamel or Velouté, whichever is the more convenient. At home you seldom use more than one sauce, or two at the most, in a meal, but it may be helpful for you to know that the one you will need – or the base for it – can be made earlier in the day and merely reheated, or combined with the cream and egg yolks as it is reheated at meal time when there are always so many things for one pair of hands to do.

The roux for these White Sauces is made by adding flour to melted butter and cooking and stirring the mixture over low heat until the mixture just starts to take on a golden colour. This is a white roux or *roux blanc*. Cooking the roux slowly is important because on this depends the desired expansion of the starch in the flour, a factor that influences the smooth texture of a sauce. Fine texture depends also upon constantly stirring the mixture after the milk or stock is added and while the sauce is thickening and upon frequently stirring it while it is being reduced.

A good recipe will give you the correct proportion of all ingredients but for a really fine sauce you must exercise judgment as well. The following pointers should prove helpful.

. . . In reducing either Béchamel or Velouté, cook down to the consistency of a heavy cream, or *à la nappe*, which means thick enough to coat the back of a spoon when it is lifted out of the saucepan. Another way of describing this is that it has *du corps*, or body, meaning that it will form a light coating, never an unappetizingly thick one, on a food.

. . . Use Parmesan for first choice and hard dry Swiss for second choice when making Mornay Sauce. They grate very fine and so disperse quickly and thoroughly in the hot mixture. Their flavour is right, too, because they will give a cheese flavour pronounced enough to be recognizable yet at the same time subtle and delicate. The flavour should complement, not overwhelm, the food that is sauced. American Cheddar, suitable for other purposes like Welsh Rarebit, is too soft and rich in fat for Mornay Sauce.

. . . A little fresh butter added to any of the sauces at the last minute gives a last fine touch. It will thicken the mixture just the least bit if the butter is combined in the hot sauce by moving the pan in a circular motion to swirl it in, and the pan is removed from the fire when the butter is not quite melted.

. . . In adding egg yolks to a hot sauce, mix them with a little cream and then stir some of the hot sauce into this mixture. Add this to the sauce (which has been removed from the heat) and stir briskly until combined. Return to the heat and cook, stirring constantly and briskly just until it comes back to a boil but do not allow to boil. This way the eggs will not coagulate and cause a curdled sauce.

. . . Finally, a perfect sauce is not finished until it is strained through a very fine sieve or cheesecloth.

Butter sauces of the Hollandaise type are considered part of the White-Sauce group. These depend upon an emulsion of egg yolks and butter instead of the flour-and-butter roux to give them their characteristic thickness. Hollandaise and Bearnaise are the two important sauces of this group and there are only a few variations. Many home cooks seem scared to attempt making either of these sauces, probably because they separate or curdle unless proper precautions are taken. Actually there is no reason why anyone should ever have a failure because the precautions are a mere three in number.

. . . Use a double boiler, keeping the water in the bottom just under the boiling point by adding to it frequently a spoonful or two of cold water.

. . . Add the butter a little at a time, making sure that each addition is completely incorporated before adding the next.

. . . Stir the sauce every minute of the time until it is finished.

If, however, you should disregard one of these warnings and the sauce does curdle, you can bring it back to a homogeneous thickness by putting a fresh egg yolk in another pan and gradually whipping in the curdled mixture.

BECHAMEL SAUCE

4 tablespoons butter
2 tablespoons finely chopped
  onion (optional)
½ cup flour

3 pints boiling milk
½ teaspoon salt
5 white peppercorns
2 sprigs parsley

Pinch of grated nutmeg (optional)

Melt butter in a saucepan, add onion, if used, and cook until it is soft but not brown. Add flour, mix well and cook slowly until the flour just starts to turn golden. Add milk, a pint at a time, stirring vigorously, preferably with a wire whip. Add salt, peppercorns, parsley and if desired, the nutmeg. Cook slowly, stirring frequently for about 30 minutes or until reduced to two thirds the original quantity and the sauce is the consistency of a very heavy cream. Strain through a fine sieve. Makes 1 quart of Béchamel. The onion is omitted if the sauce is for very delicate foods or if the flavour is not liked. Used for vegetables, fish, poultry, or any 'creamed' dish, and as the base for Mornay, Cream and other sauces.

CREAM SAUCE

1 pint Béchamel (above)
½ cup heavy cream
Few drops lemon juice

Cook the Béchamel until reduced to about 1½ cups. Add the cream and bring back to the boiling point. Add lemon juice if the sauce is for fish. Used for vegetables, fish, poultry, eggs and for any food that is served 'creamed'.

CREAM SAUCE (for Braised Veal or Chicken)

1 cup cream   *Few drops lemon juice*
1 cup Cream Sauce (page 40) or Velouté (page 41)

After removing the veal or chicken from the pan, take out all the
fat, leaving in the meat juice. Put the cream in the pan, bring to
a boil and cook, stirring constantly, until reduced one half. Add
Cream Sauce or Velouté, correct the seasoning with salt and strain
through a fine sieve. Add lemon juice if desired. The sauce should
be ivory coloured.

VELOUTE SAUCE

4 tablespoons butter   *½ teaspoon salt (unless stock is*
¼ cup flour   *salty)*
3 pints white stock (page 30)   *1 cup mushroom peelings (or*
5 white peppercorns   *stems) (if available)*

Melt butter in a saucepan, add flour, mix well and cook slowly
until it just starts to turn golden. Add boiling stock, a pint at a
time, stirring vigorously with a whip. Add remaining ingredients
and cook slowly, stirring frequently, about 1 hour, skimming from
time to time, until the mixture is cooked to two thirds its original
quantity and the sauce is the consistency of very heavy cream.
(The butter which rises to the top and is skimmed off can be
saved to sauté meat or fish.) Strain through a fine sieve. If it is to
be stored in the refrigerator, stir with a whip from time to time as
it cools. If it is too thick, it can be thinned by adding more stock.
Store in a covered jar in the refrigerator. If not used within a week,
recook it, put in a clean jar and return to the refrigerator. Used as
the base for Suprême, Allemande and other sauces and for thickening other sauces.

FISH VELOUTE Number I

3 tablespoons butter   1 quart fish stock (page 31)
3 tablespoons flour   Salt (unless stock is salty)

Melt butter in a saucepan, add flour, mix well and cook slowly until it just starts to turn golden. Add stock slowly stirring vigorously with a whip. Cook 15 to 20 minutes and strain through a fine sieve.

FISH VELOUTE Number II

When poaching fish, cook the liquor after removing the fish from the pan until reduced to about 1 cup, and thicken it with Manie Butter made by creaming together 1 tablespoon butter with 1 teaspoon flour. Bring to a boil but do not allow to boil. Correct the seasoning with salt.

MORNAY SAUCE

4 egg yolks, slightly beaten   2 tablespoons grated Parmesan
¼ cup cream   or dry Swiss cheese
1 quart hot Béchamel   1 tablespoon whipped cream
(page 40)   (optional)

Mix the egg yolks and cream and combine with the Béchamel. Cook, stirring constantly, until the boiling point is reached. Add cheese. Used for fish, vegetables, poultry, poached eggs, noodles, macaroni and other 'creamed' foods that are to be browned in the oven. Usually a little grated cheese is sprinkled over the top before browning. For a very even brown top, reserve a few spoonfuls of the sauce and fold into it the whipped cream and spread this over the top before putting in the oven or grill to brown.

SUPREME SAUCE

1 pint chicken stock
3 sliced mushrooms (or
mushroom peelings
and stems)

1 cup Velouté (page 41)
1 cup cream
Salt
Pinch of cayenne pepper

Cook stock and mushrooms until reduced to one third the original quantity. Combine with Velouté, bring to a boil and cook until reduced to about 1 cup and gradually add the cream, stirring constantly. Correct the seasoning with salt and cayenne and strain through a fine sieve or cheesecloth. If not to be used immediately, put a little butter on the top to prevent a crusty skin from forming on the surface. Used for fish, poultry, eggs and other 'creamed' mixtures.

ALLEMANDE SAUCE

2 egg yolks, slightly beaten
¼ cup cream

1 pint Supreme Sauce (above)
2 tablespoons very heavy cream

Mix the egg yolks and cream and combine with Supreme Sauce. Cook, stirring constantly, until the boiling point is reached. Add the heavy cream. This is an extremely rich sauce and is used for foods that are not too rich such as boiled chicken.

BERCY SAUCE

3 tablespoons butter
1 teaspoon finely chopped
shallots
½ cup white wine

1 teaspoon flour
¼ teaspoon salt
Pepper
1 teaspoon chopped parsley

Melt 1 tablespoon butter in a saucepan, add shallots and cook a few minutes until they are soft but not brown. Add wine and cook until reduced to ¼ cup. Add Manie Butter made by creaming together the remaining 2 tablespoons butter and the flour and cook, mixing all together until well blended. Season with salt and pepper and add parsley. Generally used for fish. The fish is placed in a fire-proof dish with the sauce spread over the top, then baked in the oven and served from the baking dish.

WHITE BERCY (for Fish)

½ cup white wine
½ cup fish stock (page 31) or water
2 teaspoons chopped shallots
1 cup Cream Sauce (page 40)

2 tablespoons butter
Chopped parsley
2 tablespoons whipped cream
(optional)

Combine wine, stock (or water) and shallots in pan for cooking fish. Put the fish in the pan and cover with a piece of buttered paper cut the size of the pan with a half-inch hole in the centre. Cover the pan, bring to the boil and cook slowly until fish is done. Remove fish to serving dish. Reduce the cooking liquid to one half the original quantity and add the Cream Sauce. Bring to a boil and add butter and parsley. Pour over fish and brown in hot oven or under grill. For a very even golden brown, add the whipped cream before pouring the sauce over the top of the fish and putting in the oven to brown.

AURORE SAUCE

3 tablespoons tomato purée
(or well-reduced Tomato
Sauce)

1 pint Béchamel (page 40) or
Mornay Sauce (page 42)
1 tablespoon butter

Add the tomato purée or sauce to the Béchamel or Mornay Sauce. Mix well and add butter. Used for poultry and eggs.

SAUCE au PLAT (for Fish)

Poach fish in white wine following directions for Filet of Sole Veronique (page 60). Remove fish to heat-proof serving dish and reduce liquor in pan until it has almost all cooked away. Add 1 cup White-Wine Sauce (page 54) or Cream Sauce (page 40), mix with liquid in pan and cook 5 minutes. Add 2 tablespoons butter and pour over fish. If dish is to be browned under the grill fold in 2 tablespoons whipped cream or 1 tablespoon Hollandaise Sauce, if any is available, as soon as butter has melted.

BONNE FEMME SAUCE (for Fish)

Follow directions for Sauce au Plat for Fish (above), adding sliced mushrooms to the pan when fish is cooking.

CAPER SAUCE

2 tablespoons capers   2 teaspoons chopped parsley
          2 cups hot Cream Sauce (page 40)

Add capers and parsley to Cream Sauce. Used for boiled or grilled fish.

CARDINAL SAUCE

Shell and coral of 1 cooked   2 cups hot Fish Velouté Number I
   lobster   or II (page 42) or hot Béchamel
3 tablespoons butter   (page 40)
3 to 4 tablespoons water   2 to 3 tablespoons milk (if needed)
          A little truffle juice (if obtainable)

Make Lobster Butter as follows: Pound and crush shell and coral of cooked lobster with butter (or grind shell in meat chopper and then crush with coral and butter). Add water and cook slowly 10 to 15 minutes. Strain through a fine sieve. Chill in refrigerator and remove butter which rises and hardens on the top. Discard water and add butter to the hot Velouté or Béchamel. If sauce is too thick, add milk as required to thin it. Add truffle juice, if used. Sauce should be pink, if not add 1 or 2 drops red vegetable colouring. Used for fish.

CHIVRY SAUCE

2 tablespoons chopped spinach leaves

1 teaspoon tarragon and chervil

½ cup white wine

1 tablespoon chopped mixed tarragon, chervil and chives

1 tablespoon chopped watercress

2 cups hot Cream Sauce (page 40)

2 tablespoons Hollandaise (optional) (page 56)

Cook spinach with teaspoonful of tarragon and chervil in a little water for a few minutes. Drain and rub through a fine sieve. Meanwhile put the wine in a saucepan with the tablespoon mixed tarragon, chervil and chives and the watercress. Cook until reduced to about one third the original quantity. Add the Cream Sauce and strain through a fine sieve. Add the strained spinach mixture to colour the sauce. If a richer sauce is desired, add the Hollandaise. Used for boiled poultry.

CURRY SAUCE

1 tablespoon butter

1 finely chopped onion

A small bay leaf

A little thyme

1 tablespoon curry powder

¼ cup white stock

1½ cups Velouté (page 41)

½ cup cream

Melt butter in saucepan, add onion and cook until soft but not brown. Add bay leaf, thyme and curry powder. Mix well. Add stock and bring to the boil. Add Velouté and cook 10 to 15 minutes. Strain through a fine sieve, add cream and bring back to the boil. Used for meat, fish, shellfish, poultry, eggs.

EGG SAUCE

2 chopped hard-boiled eggs   1 pint hot Cream Sauce
½ teaspoon chopped parsley   (page 40)
        1 tablespoon Hollandaise (optional) (page 56)

Add eggs and parsley to Cream Sauce. If a richer sauce is desired, fold in the Hollandaise. Used for boiled or grilled fish.

LIVORNIENNE SAUCE

1 tablespoon chopped green   1 tablespoon chopped
    lettuce leaves   parsley
2 tablespoons cooked carrot,   1 tablespoon julienne of
    cut in julienne   truffles
        1 pint hot White-Wine Sauce (pages 54–55)

Parboil the lettuce leaves for 5 minutes and drain well. Add to White-Wine Sauce along with remaining ingredients. Used for fish.

MUSTARD SAUCE

1 teaspoon English mustard   1 cup hot Cream Sauce (page 40)
1 tablespoon water   1 tablespoon Hollandaise (optional)

Mix mustard and water and combine with Cream Sauce. If a richer sauce is desired fold in the Hollandaise. Used for fish.

MARINIERE SAUCE

Follow directions for Poulette Sauce (page 51) omitting the mushrooms. Used for fish.

MATELOTE SAUCE

3 tablespoons butter	Peelings of mushrooms
1 finely chopped onion	Chopped fish head and
1 finely chopped carrot	bones (salmon or sole
A little thyme	preferred)
1 bay leaf	1 quart red or white wine
1 clove garlic	1 teaspoon flour

Melt 1 tablespoon butter in a saucepan, add onion and carrot and cook slowly until golden. Add thyme, bay leaf, garlic, mushroom peelings and fish head and bones. Add a little water and simmer 10 minutes. Add wine, cover pan and cook until reduced to 1 pint. Strain through a fine sieve. Add Manie Butter made by creaming together 1 tablespoon butter with the flour. Mix well and bring back to the boil. Add remaining tablespoon butter. Used for fish.

MUSHROOM CREAM SAUCE

2 tablespoons butter	¼ cup Velouté (page 41) or
¼ pound small mushrooms,	Cream Sauce (page 40)
cleaned and peeled	Salt
1 cup cream	Pepper

Melt butter in saucepan, add mushrooms and cook until lightly browned. Add cream and cook 6 to 8 minutes. Add Velouté or Cream Sauce and season with salt and pepper. Used for poultry, sweetbreads and fish.

NORMANDE SAUCE

2 tablespoons butter
1 teaspoon flour
1 cup liquid (some liquor from fish, oysters or mussels for which the sauce will be used

and liquor from cooking mushrooms that will garnish the dish)
2 egg yolks, slightly beaten
½ cup cream

Melt butter in a saucepan, add flour and cook until it just starts to turn golden. Add liquid and cook about 10 minutes. Mix egg yolks and cream and combine with sauce. Bring back to the boil, stirring constantly, but do not allow to boil. Strain through a fine sieve and pour over the fish. Used for fish, oysters and mussels.

NEWBURG SAUCE Number I

1½ pound live lobster
Salt and pepper
3 tablespoons butter
1 teaspoon chopped shallots (or onion)
1 glass (5 ounces) Sherry
1 cup medium cream

¼ cup Cream Sauce (page 40) (or Velouté) (page 41) or a roux made with 1 tablespoon butter and 1 teaspoon flour
2 egg yolks
½ cup heavy cream

Cut lobster into about 4 pieces and crack the claws (the claw meat can be removed more easily from a cooked lobster if claws are cracked a bit before cooking). Season with a little salt. Melt 2 tablespoons butter in a saucepan, add lobster and sauté for about 4 minutes. Add the shallots, one half of the Sherry and the medium cream. Cover pan, bring to a boil and let cook 20 to 25 minutes. Remove lobster and cook liquid in pan until reduced to about one half the original quantity. Add Cream Sauce (or Velouté) or the roux of butter and flour made by melting the butter, adding the flour and cooking the mixture until it just starts to turn golden. Mix all together with a whip and let cook 10 to 15 minutes. Beat egg yolks slightly and mix with heavy cream and combine with sauce by adding a little hot sauce to egg-yolk mixture and then pouring this back into the hot sauce, stirring briskly all the time. Bring back to a boil but do not allow to boil. Add remaining half of the Sherry and correct the seasoning with salt and freshly ground white pepper. Strain through a fine sieve or cheesecloth. Remove lobster meat from shells and combine with sauce. Used for fish and shellfish.

NEWBURG SAUCE Number II

2 or 3 fresh lobsters
2 tablespoons butter
1 teaspoon chopped shallot
  (or onion)
1½ cups medium cream

1 teaspoon flour
½ teaspoon salt
1 or 2 egg yolks
¼ cup heavy cream
1 glass (4 ounces) Sherry

Remove small claws from lobsters and set aside. Boil lobsters in salted water that covers them well for 20 minutes. Remove from water, and when cool enough to handle, discard sac behind head and dark vein along the back. Remove meat from tail, body and large claws, cut in pieces and put in a saucepan with a little butter. Cover pan and set where it will just keep a little warm. Melt one tablespoon of the butter in a pan, add shallot (or onion) and cook until soft. Cut into small pieces the small claws that were set aside, break up all the shells from the cooked lobsters in small pieces and add to the butter and shallot in pan. Add medium cream and cook slowly about 20 minutes. Strain. Melt the other tablespoon butter in a saucepan, add flour and cook until it starts to turn golden. Add the strained lobster-flavoured cream and cook stirring constantly until well blended and slightly thickened. Season with salt. Combine egg yolks with heavy cream and add a little of the hot sauce, then stir the mixture into the sauce. Add Sherry and bring back to a boil but do not allow to boil. Combine with lobster meat over a very low heat, being careful the mixture does not boil. Another 2 ounces of Sherry may be added if desired.

NANTUA SAUCE

12 or more cooked crawfish
shells from which the meat
has been removed

3 tablespoons butter
3 tablespoons water
½ cup cream

2 cups Béchamel (page 40)

Make crawfish butter as follows: Pound and crush the shells with
the butter and cook slowly with the water for 10 or 15 minutes.
Strain through a fine sieve. Chill in refrigerator and remove butter
which rises and hardens on the top. Mix this butter and cream
with the hot Béchamel Sauce. The sauce should be pink; if not,
add 2 drops of red vegetable colour. Used for fish or eggs.

PAPRIKA or HUNGROISE SAUCE

1 tablespoon butter
1 finely chopped onion
2 tablespoons paprika
Salt

6 tablespoons Velouté (page
41) or Cream Sauce (page
40)
1 cup cream

Melt butter in a saucepan, add onion and cook until golden. Add
paprika and mix well. Add cream gradually and continue cooking,
stirring constantly. Add Velouté or Cream Sauce. Correct the
seasoning with salt. Used for fish, poultry and veal.

POULETTE SAUCE

1 tablespoon butter
6 to 8 sliced mushrooms
2 teaspoons finely chopped
shallots
1 glass (4 ounces) white wine
¾ cup cream

½ cup Béchamel (page 40) or
Cream Sauce (page 40)
Salt
2 egg yolks, slightly beaten
½ teaspoon lemon juice
½ teaspoon chopped parsley

Melt butter in a saucepan, add mushrooms and cook until they just start to turn brown. Add shallots and wine and cook until wine is reduced to almost nothing. Add ¼ cup cream. Cook until reduced to one half the original quantity and add Béchamel or Cream Sauce. Bring to the boil and correct the seasoning with salt. Mix egg yolks with remaining ¼ cup of cream, combine with sauce and bring back to the boil, stirring constantly, but do not allow to boil. Add lemon juice and parsley. Used for fish, shellfish, calf's brains and other specialties.

HOT RAVIGOTE SAUCE

⅓ cup white wine
⅓ cup vinegar
2 teaspoons finely chopped shallots

1 pint hot Cream Sauce (page 40) or Sauce Blanche (page 56)

Put wine, vinegar and shallots in a saucepan and cook until reduced to one third the original quantity. Add Cream Sauce or Sauce Blanche. Used for boiled poultry and fish.

SHALLOT SAUCE

1 tablespoon chopped shallots
¾ cup white wine
2 tablespoons butter

1½ cups Velouté (page 41)
1 teaspoon lemon juice

Put shallots and wine in a saucepan and cook until reduced to about 2 tablespoons. Add Velouté and cook slowly 5 minutes. Remove from fire, add lemon juice and butter. Used for fish.

SMITANE SAUCE

1 glass (4 ounces) white wine
(or 2 tablespoons vinegar)

1 tablespoon beef extract
(or veal gravy)

Few drops lemon juice   1 cup Cream Sauce (page 40)
White pepper and salt   1 teaspoon chopped shallots

Put shallots and wine (or vinegar) in a saucepan and cook until reduced to almost nothing. Add beef extract (or veal gravy) and bring to a boil. Add Cream Sauce, bring to a boil mixing all together well. Add lemon juice and correct the seasoning with salt and pepper. Strain. Used for meat and poultry and feathered game.

SOUBISE SAUCE

1 cup chopped onions   1 pint Béchamel Sauce (page 40)
1 tablespoon butter   1 cup cream
             Salt

Cover onions with hot water, bring to the boil and cook 3 to 4 minutes. Drain. Put onions in saucepan with butter and cook slowly until soft but not brown. Add Béchamel and cook 15 minutes. Strain through a fine sieve, return to the heat and add cream, little by little. Correct the seasoning with salt. Used for fish, lamb, veal or sweetbreads.

SOUR CREAM SAUCE
(for Roast Veal or Poultry)

2 tablespoons vinegar   1 cup Cream Sauce (page 40)
1 cup medium heavy cream   Salt
        A little lemon juice (optional)

When meat is done, remove from roasting pan and pour off all the fat from the pan. Add vinegar and cook until reduced to 1 tablespoon. Add cream and cook, stirring constantly, until reduced to one half the original quantity. Add Cream Sauce, bring to the boil and cook 10 to 15 minutes. Strain through a fine sieve and correct the seasoning with salt. If a sharper flavour is desired, add lemon juice. Used for roast veal and roast poultry.

VENITIENNE SAUCE

1 tablespoon vinegar
½ cup white wine
1 teaspoon chopped shallot
A little chopped tarragon,
    parsley and chervil

1 pint Cream Sauce (page 40)
2 tablespoons butter
1 teaspoon finely chopped
    tarragon and chervil
1 cup finely chopped watercress

Put vinegar, wine, shallot, tarragon, parsley and chervil in a sauce-pan and cook until reduced to almost nothing. Add Cream Sauce, cook a few minutes longer and strain through a fine sieve or cheese-cloth. Meanwhile cream the butter with the chopped tarragon, chervil and watercress and rub through a fine sieve. Add to the sauce to give it a light-green colour. Used for fish.

VILLEROY SAUCE

3 cups Velouté (page 41) 2 egg yolks, slightly beaten. Cook Velouté until reduced to 2 cups (should be very thick). Combine with egg yolks and cook until it reaches the boiling point, stirring constantly, but do not allow to boil. Cool to lukewarm before using. Used when chicken, lamb, sweetbreads or vegetables are to be fried in deep fat or when making croquettes. The food is coated with the sauce and then prepared for deep fat frying by dipping in beaten egg and then in fine dry bread crumbs. In the case of croquettes, the food is finely minced and mixed with the sauce and formed into pyramids or other shapes.

WHITE-WINE SAUCE (for Fish)

3 tablespoons butter
½ teaspoon salt
2 chopped shallots
½ cup mushroom peelings

½ cup fish stock (page 31)
1 cup Cream Sauce (page 40)
    or Velouté (page 41)
½ cup cream

¼ cup white wine   Salt and pepper
Few drops lemon juice

Put 1 tablespoon butter, salt, shallots and mushroom peelings in a shallow pan. Place fish on top and add wine and fish stock. Cover with a piece of buttered paper cut the size of the pan with a small hole in the centre. Cover pan and cook until the fish is done. Remove fish to serving dish. Cook liquid in pan until reduced to one third its original quantity. Add Cream Sauce or Velouté and cream and bring back to the boil. Add butter, correct seasoning with salt, pepper and add lemon juice. Strain over fish.

BEARNAISE SAUCE

3 sprigs tarragon   ¼ cup white wine (optional)
3 sprigs chervil   3 egg yolks
1 teaspoon chopped shallots   1 tablespoon water
4 crushed peppercorns   ½ pound butter (soft)
¼ cup vinegar   ¼ teaspoon salt
Very little cayenne pepper

Remove leaves from tarragon and chervil (save to finish the sauce) and chop the stems. Put in a saucepan with shallots, peppercorns and vinegar and wine (if it is used). Cook all together until reduced to a thick paste. Put the egg yolks, water and the paste in top of a double boiler and stir briskly with a wire whip or slotted spoon until light and fluffy. Add a little cold water to bottom of double boiler to keep water below the boiling point and do this frequently while making the sauce. Add a few spoonfuls of butter and stir constantly until the butter is melted and the sauce starts to thicken. Add a little more butter and continue stirring until it is melted and incorporated in the sauce. Continue adding butter and stirring constantly until all has been added. Season to taste with salt and cayenne pepper. Strain through a fine sieve and add the chopped leaves of tarragon and chervil. Used for grilled steak and fish.

HOLLANDAISE SAUCE

3 egg yolks	¼ teaspoon salt
1 tablespoon water	½ teaspoon lemon juice
½ pound butter (soft)	1 tablespoon hot water (optional)

Put egg yolks and water in top of a double boiler and stir briskly with a wire whip or slotted spoon until light and fluffy. Add a little cold water to bottom of boiler to keep water below the boiling point and do this frequently while making the sauce. Add a few spoonfuls of the butter and stir constantly until the butter is melted and sauce starts to thicken. Add a little more butter and continue stirring until it is melted and incorporated in the sauce. Continue adding butter and stirring constantly until all has been added. Add salt. If the sauce is for fish, add the lemon juice. The hot water is added if a lighter sauce is desired. Used for fish, vegetables and eggs.

SAUCE BLANCHE (A Substitute for Hollandaise)

2 to 3 tablespoons butter	A little white pepper
1 tablespoon flour	2 egg yolks, slightly beaten
1 cup boiling water	¼ cup light cream
¼ teaspoon salt	½ teaspoon lemon juice

Melt 1 tablespoon of the butter in a saucepan, add flour and mix together without cooking. Add water, salt and pepper and mix all together well. Mix egg yolks with cream, add a little of the sauce mixture and then combine with the remaining sauce in the pan. Cook, stirring vigorously until the boiling point is reached but do not boil. Add lemon juice and remaining 2 or more tablespoons of butter, swirling it in by moving the pan in a circular motion and removing from the heat when the butter is not quite melted. Used for vegetables, fish and any foods with which Hollandaise is usually served.

MALTAISE SAUCE

When Hollandaise Sauce (page 56) is ready to serve, add 2 or 3 tablespoons orange juice of good colour and a little finely grated orange rind. Should be pink coloured, and 1 or 2 drops pink vegetable colouring may be added if desired. Used for asparagus.

MOUSSELINE SAUCE

Just before serving, add 2 tablespoons whipped cream to 1 cup Hollandaise Sauce (page 56). Used for asparagus, broccoli, artichokes, salmon or any food for which Hollandaise is used.

CHORON SAUCE

1 cup Bearnaise Sauce (page 55)
¼ cup tomato purée (or Tomato Sauce (page 70) that has been cooked until reduced very thick)

Combine the Bearnaise Sauce and tomato purée (or thick Tomato Sauce). Used for meat, chicken or fish.

SUBSTITUTE BEARNAISE

2 stalks tarragon
2 stalks chervil
1 teaspoon chopped shallots
2 tablespoons vinegar

½ cup Béchamel Sauce
(page 40)
1 egg yolk, lightly beaten
¼ cup butter

Remove leaves from tarragon and chervil stalks, chop leaves and set aside to add later. Put stems and shallots in vinegar and cook until reduced to almost nothing. Add Béchamel Sauce and cook a few minutes. Combine with egg yolk without allowing sauce to boil after adding it. Add butter, a little at a time, combining each addition thoroughly before adding the next. Strain through a fine sieve and add finely chopped tarragon and chervil leaves.

SUBSTITUTE HOLLANDAISE

2 egg yolks, beaten
Few drops lemon juice
1 teaspoon cold water

½ cup hot Béchamel Sauce
(page 40)
¼ cup butter

Mix together egg yolks, lemon juice and water. Add Béchamel Sauce. Heat slowly, stirring constantly, removing from heat as soon as it starts to boil. Add butter a little at a time, combining each addition before adding the next. Correct the seasoning.

VALOIS SAUCE

To 1 cup Bearnaise Sauce (page 55) add 1 teaspoon melted beef extract to give a light brownish colour. Used for eggs or grilled chicken.

The following recipes are examples of dishes
sauced the French way with White Sauces.

CHICKEN SAUTE GLORIA SWANSON

1 young chicken (2½ to 3 pounds)
2 cups cooked rice
¼ teaspoon salt
A little pepper
2 tablespoons butter
8 mushrooms
1 teaspoon finely chopped
  shallots (or onion)

1 tablespoon flour
1 glass (4 ounces) white wine
1 faggot made by tying together
  3 sprigs parsley ½ bay leaf, a
  little thyme
1 cup cream (or top milk)
2 egg yolks
8 tomatoes

Clean chicken and cut in pieces, legs, second joints, breasts and wings. Season with salt and pepper. Melt butter in large pan and when hot add chicken. Cook the pieces until golden brown, about 5 or 6 minutes on each side. Clean mushrooms, add to the pan and cook another 4 or 5 minutes. Add shallots (or onions) to the pan, sprinkle in the flour mixing it in well with mushrooms and shallots and cook a few minutes longer. Add wine and ½ cup of the cream (or top milk). Bring to a boil combining thoroughly with shallots and mushrooms. Add faggot, cover pan partially and cook slowly about 25 to 35 minutes or until chicken is done. Remove faggot. Mix egg yolks with remaining cream and combine with sauce in pan (by adding a little hot sauce to egg-yolk mixture and then turning that back into pan, shaking and moving pan with the heat turned off until well combined). Correct seasoning with salt and white pepper. For the garnish, peel and seed 8 halves of tomatoes and cook a few minutes in oven or in a little butter in a saucepan, and mould hot Rice Pilau in small buttered cups (demi-tasse size). Alternate rice moulds, each garnished with a slice of truffle and tomatoes sprinkled with parsley around chicken and pour sauce over. Serves four.

CHICKEN SAUTE HELENE

3 to 4 pound chicken	1 cup chicken stock (or water)
2 tablespoons butter	2 to 3 cups cooked rice
1 onion chopped	1 tablespoon curry powder
1 teaspoon flour	½ cup heavy cream
½ clove garlic, crushed	3 apples (for garnish)

Clean and singe chicken and cut in 8 pieces (legs and second joints, wings, breasts and back). Season with salt. Melt butter in saucepan and when hot arrange pieces of chicken in it and cook until golden brown on both sides. Add onion, cover pan and continue cooking until onions start to get soft. Add garlic, sprinkle in the flour and curry powder and mix well. Add stock (or water), bring to a boil and cook 35 to 40 minutes or until chicken is tender and no pink juice follows fork when withdrawn from second joint to test it. Remove pieces of chicken to serving dish, reduce sauce if there is more than ½ cup in pan, stirring in all the juice cooked on side of pan. Add cream, bring to a boil. Correct seasoning with salt and pour over chicken. While chicken is cooking, peel and core apples and cut in quarters, dip in flour and sauté in butter until soft. Garnish dish with sautéed apples and serve Rice Pilau separately. Serves four to five.

FILET OF SOLE (or other Fish) VERONIQUE

3 tablespoons butter
1 teaspoon chopped shallot (or onion)
4 fillets of sole (or other fish)
¼ teaspoon salt
1 glass (5 ounces) white wine
½ cup White-Wine Sauce (pages 54–55) (or Cream Sauce, page 40)

2 tablespoons whipped cream (or 1 of Hollandaise and 1 of whipped cream) (optional)
A little pepper
1 cup seedless grapes (fresh or canned)

Melt 1 tablespoon butter in shallow pan, add shallots (or onion). Season fish with salt and arrange on top of butter and shallots. Sprinkle wine over fish. Cover with a piece of buttered paper cut the size of the pan with a half-inch hole in the centre, then place cover on pan. Bring to a boil and simmer 10 to 12 minutes. Remove fish to heat-proof serving dish. Cook the liquor until reduced to one third the original quantity and add White-Wine Sauce (or Cream Sauce) that has been mixed with the remaining 2 tablespoons of butter. Strain through a fine sieve. Correct the seasoning with salt and freshly ground pepper and fold in whipped cream (or Hollandaise and whipped cream). If fresh grapes are used poach for a few minutes in water and drain. Place grapes around fish and pour the sauce over. Brown under a hot grill or in a hot oven, placing the dish on a cold pan to prevent the sauce boiling while the top is browning. The whipped cream (or Hollandaise and whipped cream) may be omitted but this gives a more even golden-brown glaze. Serves four.

FILET OF SOLE
(or other Fish) BONNE FEMME

Follow directions for Filet of Sole Veronique, omitting the grapes and adding 8 sliced mushrooms and 1 teaspoon of parsley to the butter and shallots in the pan, and increasing the butter to 2 tablespoons. Do not strain this sauce.

BRAISED STUFFED BREAST OF VEAL
DOMINICAINE

STUFFING

2 pounds spinach	A little pepper
2 tablespoons butter	½ cup fresh bread crumbs
1 tablespoon chopped onion	2 cups cooked rice
½ teaspoon salt	1 egg, beaten

1 teaspoon chopped parsley

Clean spinach, parboil, drain well and chop coarsely. Heat the butter in saucepan, add chopped onion and cook until soft but not brown. Add the spinach, season with salt and pepper and heat well. Remove pan from heat and add the bread crumbs, cooked rice, parsley and egg. Mix well and correct the seasoning with salt and pepper.

1 breast of veal	1 cup cream
1 sliced onion	1 cup Cream Sauce (page 40)
1 sliced carrot	(or Velouté, page 41)
1 tablespoon butter (or good fat)	Few drops lemon juice

Have the butcher cut a pocket in the breast of veal and stuff with the mixture above. Sew the edges of the pocket together. Cover the bottom of a casserole with onion and carrot mixed with butter (or good fat). Place the stuffed breast on top and cook in a medium oven of 400 degrees, basting often with the butter and the juice that cooks out of the veal until well browned. Add about ¼ cup water to the casserole, cover and cook until the meat is tender, about 2 to 2½ hours. Remove meat from casserole. Skim off the fat and add 1 cup of cream to liquid in pan. Cook until reduced to a third of the original quantity. Strain through a fine sieve into another pan. Add 1 cup of Cream Sauce (or Velouté Sauce). Bring to a boil, blending thoroughly. Add lemon juice and correct seasoning with salt and a little freshly ground white pepper. If too thick, add a little more cream. Cut meat in slices and serve with sauce.

III. BROWN SAUCES

III. BROWN SAUCES

THE Brown Sauces have always played a great role in French cooking. They are recognized by their rich brown or red-brown colour that comes from a brown roux usually in combination with brown stock, sometimes from tomatoes (fresh, canned, purée or sauce) that are added and often from the addition of good red wine. They have a fine rich flavour that results from a blending of these ingredients with seasonings and herbs and such vegetables as onions, shallots and mushrooms in scores of combinations. Brown Sauces are nourishing but are less fattening than the White Sauces because they are not enriched with cream or cheese, and when properly made they are not indigestible because they are never heavy with fat and never overthick with flour, which tends to hold excess fat in a sauce.

Brown Sauces can be made in several ways. For example, they can be made right in the pan in which meat has been roasted or sautéed and they can be made by cooking the liquid right with the meat as in stews. But the really fine sauces in the Brown-Sauce group derive their superiority from the inclusion of one or more of the three basic ones, Brown Sauce, Tomato Sauce and Demiglacé, also called Espagnole. I believe that anyone who can make

65

a really good Brown Sauce, an equally good Tomato Sauce and a fine Espagnole is well on the way to becoming a skilled *saucier*. In the kitchens of large hotels these three sauces are always on the range ready to be incorporated into the many famous sauces that are served with the various entrées. At home they can be made occasionally and kept in readiness in the refrigerator.

Brown Sauces are thickened with a brown roux, *le roux brun*. This is a mixture of equal parts of fat and flour cooked together until it takes on a deep brown – a hazelnut brown – colour. The importance of slow cooking and constant stirring and the use of a heavy metal pan cannot be overemphasized in making a brown roux because it is so easy for it to scorch or to take on a spotty brown that indicates partial scorching. And a scorched roux always imparts an unpleasant bitter taste to a sauce. It may interest those who are on fat-free diets that it is perfectly possible to use browned flour (as described on page 69) for thickening a Brown Sauce and thus include no fat at all.

An even larger amount of liquid is added to the roux in making Brown Sauces than is customary in making White Sauces. The liquid is then cooked down gradually, a process spoken of as 'the reduction'. As the mixture 'reduces', the flavours of the liquids are concentrated and the flavours of all the ingredients are thoroughly blended. At the same time excess fat and insoluble particles in the mixture rise to the top and are skimmed off. The result is the fine, smooth texture, the excellent well-rounded flavour and the glossy appearance that characterizes well-made French Brown Sauces.

Of course, in a home kitchen there are often times when a recipe calls for the addition of Brown Sauce or of Tomato Sauce or both and they are not on hand. It is possible to make a sauce that will be entirely satisfactory without them, although it won't be as fine a sauce as if it included them. For example, in making Madeira Sauce without Brown Sauce, the way to do it is to include some brown roux and use water or stock for the liquid in place of Brown Sauce. Added flavour can be achieved by cooking a little chopped shallot or onion in the fat when making this roux. As a substitute for Tomato Sauce, as for example in Portugaise

Sauce, add tomato purée or tomato juice in place of the Tomato Sauce called for in the recipe and then finish the sauce with Manie Butter (page 27).

The following pointers will prove helpful in making really fine Brown Sauces.

... Brown Sauces must always be stirred carefully, never whipped briskly because this lightens the colour and makes a less attractive sauce.

... When a recipe calls for a final finish with butter it should not be stirred in because this lightens the colour of the sauce. The pan is moved in a circular motion so that the butter is swirled in and then taken from the heat when it is barely melted. This thickens the sauce a bit as well as flavours it.

... In making Tomato Sauce watch it more carefully and stir more frequently during cooking and reducing because the weight of the ingredients encourages easy scorching.

... Brown Sauce and Tomato Sauce can be stored in covered jars in the refrigerator for a week – or longer if they are recooked at the end of a week and returned to the freshly washed jar. They can be kept longer if the top is covered with a thin layer of Sherry.

... Demi-glacé or Espagnole is used as the base for the very richest sauces and the most elegant dishes that are served with the darker meats and such foods as truffles, mushrooms and foie gras.

... An inferior wine will spoil an otherwise good sauce. An in-expensive wine can be used if it is a good wine. How fine it should be depends upon how it is incorporated into the sauce. If the wine is to reduce to almost nothing in the first steps of making the sauce it need not be so fine. If it is part of the liquid to be reduced with the other liquid it should be a better wine. If added at the end, as in Madeira Sauce, it should be a really fine wine.

... When stock or Brown Sauce is unavailable to use in a recipe, a bouillon cube or leftover meat gravy used with water will supply the lack.

BROWN SAUCE

½ cup fat (fresh, unsalted beef, veal or pork drippings but not chicken fat)
1 carrot coarsely chopped
2 onions coarsely chopped
½ cup flour
10 peppercorns
2 quarts brown stock (page 30)

1 clove garlic
A faggot made by tying together 2 stalks celery, 3 sprigs parsley, a little thyme and a small bay leaf
½ cup Tomato Sauce (page 70) (or ½ cup tomato purée or juice)

Melt fat in a heavy saucepan, add carrots and onions and cook until they start to turn golden, shaking the pan so they will cook evenly. Add flour and cook, stirring frequently, until the flour takes on a good brown colour (hazelnut brown) and the carrots and onions are also brown. Add 3 cups of the boiling stock, the garlic and the faggot. Cook, stirring until the mixture thickens, then add 3 more cups of stock. Cook very slowly, stirring occasionally, until the mixture is reduced to about 3 cups (this should take about 1 to 1½ hours). As it cooks, the excess fat will be constantly rising to the surface and should be skimmed off. Add Tomato Sauce (or purée or juice) and cook a few minutes longer. Strain through a fine sieve. Add remaining 2 cups of stock and continue cooking slowly until the sauce is reduced to about 4 cups (this should take about 1 hour), skimming the surface from time to time as needed. Strain again. Cool, stirring occasionally. Store in a covered jar in the refrigerator. If not used within a week, recook it, put in a clean jar and return to refrigerator. A little good fat melted over the top will seal it and help to keep it longer.

For a richer sauce, cook ¼ cup diced fat salt pork along with the carrots and onions. Then when adding the final 2 cups of stock also add ½ cup beef gravy or juice from roast beef.

This is the basic Brown Sauce that is used as an ingredient in a great many of the sauces in the Brown-Sauce and Game-Sauce groups. It is also used in making dishes such as hash and steak and kidney pie.

BROWN SAUCE (without fat)

5 cups brown stock (page 30)   *1 onion coarsely chopped*
¾ cup flour   *A faggot made by tying together*
1 cup Tomato Sauce (page 70)   *   3 sprigs parsley, 2 stalks celery,*
* (or tomato purée or juice or*   *   a little thyme and ½ bay leaf*
* fresh tomatoes)*   *10 peppercorns*
1 carrot coarsely chopped   *1 clove garlic*

Bring the stock to a boil. Meanwhile put flour in a pan and place
in oven or under grill to brown, stirring often until the flour takes
on a good, even golden brown. Combine with the stock in a heavy
saucepan, mixing with a whip until thoroughly blended. Put the
carrot and onion in a pan and brown in oven or under grill, shaking
the pan occasionally to brown them as well as is possible on all
sides. Add them to the thickened stock along with the remaining
ingredients and cook slowly 1½ to 2 hours. (If any leftover chicken
bones are on hand, add them, too.) If sauce seems to get too thick,
add a little more stock. Strain through a fine sieve, bring back to a
boil and correct seasoning. Store in a covered jar in the refrigerator.
If not used within a week, recook, and put in a clean jar and return
to the refrigerator. Use in any recipe calling for Brown Sauce.

DEMI-GLACE SAUCE or ESPAGNOLE

Stems and peelings of   *2 cups Brown Sauce*
* mushrooms*   *1 tablespoon beef extract or*
1 glass (3 ounces) dry Sherry   * glacé-de-viande*

Chop stems and peelings of mushrooms and put in saucepan with
Sherry. Cook until reduced about one half. Add Brown Sauce and
beef extract (or glacé-de-viande). Bring to the boil and cook slowly
about 15 to 20 minutes. Used for filet mignon or other fine cut of
beef, for ham or for any meat with which Madeira Sauce is usually
served.

TOMATO SAUCE

3 tablespoons butter
1 small carrot, coarsely chopped
1 onion, coarsely chopped
¼ cup flour
1 #2½ can tomatoes or 2½ cups chopped fresh ones
1½ cups white stock (or water)
2 tablespoons sugar

2 cloves crushed garlic
A faggot made by tying together 3 sprigs parsley, 2 stalks celery, a little thyme and a small bay leaf
1 teaspoon salt
A little pepper

Melt butter in a heavy saucepan, add carrot and onion and cook until the onion is soft but not brown. Add flour and cook, stirring occasionally, until it starts to turn golden. Add remaining ingredients except sugar, bring to a boil and cook, stirring constantly, until it thickens. Continue cooking very slowly 1 to 1½ hours or until the sauce is reduced to about 1 pint, stirring occasionally and skimming the surface when necessary. Discard the faggot from sauce and strain. Add sugar. Bring back to a boil and cook 4 or 5 minutes more, stirring constantly. Store in a covered jar in the refrigerator. Used for the sauces served on macaroni, spaghetti and rice dishes, for flavouring and thickening the sauces on stews, or for any dishes where a tomato flavour is desirable.

AMERICAINE SAUCE

1 live lobster (1½ to 2 pounds)
1 finely chopped carrot
1 finely chopped onion
A little thyme
1 bay leaf

1 sprig parsley
3 tablespoons butter
¼ cup olive or salad oil
2 teaspoons chopped shallots
1 glass (4 ounces) white wine

1 pony (2 ounces) brandy
1 cup Tomato Sauce (page 70)
  (or tomato purée)
3 tomatoes, peeled, seeded and
  chopped

¼ cup fish stock (if available)
A little crushed garlic
¼ teaspoon chopped tarragon
  and chervil (if available)
Salt and pepper

Cut lobster in 8 pieces (tail in 4 pieces, the body split in 2 pieces and the claws), but remove tomalley and set it aside to thicken and finish the sauce. Prepare a Bordelaise mirepoix in a saucepan by cooking carrot, onion, thyme, bay leaf and parsley in 1 tablespoon butter until lightly browned. In another pan, heat the oil until very hot, put the lobster in it, season with salt and sauté about 5 minutes or until the meat starts to become firm. Remove lobster and place in saucepan on top of the mirepoix. Add 1 tablespoon butter, shallots and wine. Pour the brandy over this, ignite and let burn until it burns away. Add Tomato Sauce (or purée), tomatoes and stock (if used). Cover pan closely and cook 20 to 25 minutes. Remove lobster to serving dish, either in the shell or remove from shell as preferred. Strain sauce through a fine sieve and thicken by adding tomalley which was reserved and to which has been added 1 tablespoon butter, the garlic, tarragon and chervil. Do not boil sauce after adding tomalley. Correct the seasoning with salt and a little pepper and pour over lobster. Used primarily for lobster but may be used to sauce many fish. If a little thicker sauce is desired ¼ teaspoon flour can be mixed in with the tomalley and butter.

AU GRATIN SAUCE

1 teaspoon finely chopped shallots
1 glass (3 ounces) white wine
1 cup Brown Sauce (page 68)

4 tablespoons Mushroom
  Duxelles (page 32)
1 teaspoon chopped parsley

Put shallots and wine in a saucepan and cook until reduced to almost nothing. Add Brown Sauce and Mushroom Duxelles and boil 5 minutes. Add parsley. Used for fish, or for vegetables such as artichoke bottoms, braised celery or eggplant.

BORDELAISE SAUCE

2 teaspoons finely chopped
   shallots
1 glass (4 ounces) red wine

1 cup Brown Sauce (page 68)
2 tablespoons beef marrow
½ teaspoon chopped parsley

Put shallots and wine in a saucepan and cook until reduced to about three fourths the original quantity. Add Brown Sauce and cook about 10 minutes. Just before serving add beef marrow which has been cut in small dice, placed in lukewarm water for a few minutes and drained. (When purchasing marrow bone, have butcher split it so that you can remove the marrow easily.) Add parsley. Used for steak.

CURRY SAUCE (for Chicken or Lamb)

2 tablespoons butter
1 cup chopped onions
2 to 2½ pounds diced, uncooked
   lamb (or a 3 to 3½ pound
   young chicken)
1 teaspoon salt
2 crushed bay leaves
1 clove crushed garlic
A little thyme
2 to 3 tablespoons curry powder

1 quart stock (more or less) (page
   30) or water
2 tablespoons Tomato Sauce
   (page 70) or tomato purée
2 tablespoons grated coco-nut
1 green apple, peeled, cored and
   chopped
3 tablespoons arrowroot (or
   cornflour)
½ cup cream

Melt butter in saucepan, add onions and cook until lightly browned. Remove fat and sinews from lamb, season with salt and add to butter and onions. Add bay leaves, garlic, thyme, and curry powder, mix well and add stock (or water) having sufficient to cover the meat and Tomato Sauce (or purée). Bring to a boil and cook slowly for about 2 hours or until meat is tender. Remove meat to serving dish. To the sauce in the pan, add coco-nut, green apple and the arrowroot (or cornflour) mixed with a little cold water. Bring to a boil stirring all the time. Add cream, correct the seasoning with salt and pour over the lamb.

For curried chicken, substitute the chicken for the lamb. Cut chicken into eight pieces (wings, legs, second joints, breast in 3 pieces of centre and 2 sides, and back in 1 or 2 pieces), cooking it with the butter and onions about 40 minutes or until the chicken is tender. Add a little more cream because Curry Sauce for chicken should be lighter in colour.

CREOLE SAUCE

2 tablespoons butter or
 salad oil
1 onion, chopped
¼ cup chopped celery
¼ cup chopped green pepper

¼ cup chopped pimiento
3 cups canned tomatoes
1 tablespoon cornflour
2 tablespoons water
Salt and pepper

1 tablespoon chopped parsley

Melt butter (or heat oil), add onion and cook until golden. Add celery, pepper and pimiento. Add tomatoes. Bring to a boil and simmer 1 hour. Mix cornflour with water and add. Cook until sauce is thickened. Correct seasoning with salt and pepper and add parsley. Used for shellfish.

CHATEAU SAUCE
or BEURRE NOISETTE

2 tablespoons finely chopped
 shallots
1 glass (3 ounces) white wine

2 cups Demi-glacé Sauce (page 69)
¼ pound butter
1 teaspoon chopped parsley

Put shallots and wine in a saucepan and cook until reduced to almost nothing. Add Demi-glacé Sauce and cook slowly about 10 minutes. Remove from heat to side of range and add butter, stirring it in briskly with a whip to give the sauce a light-brown colour. If sauce gets too thick, add ¼ teaspoon or more of water, whipping it in. Strain. Add parsley. Used for light meats like escalope of veal, supreme or noisette of lamb, breast of chicken or escalope of sweetbread.

CHASSEUR SAUCE

1 pound mushrooms
2 tablespoons butter
¼ teaspoon salt
A little pepper
2 teaspoons chopped shallots

1 glass (4 ounces) white wine
1 cup Brown Sauce (page 68)
2 tablespoons Tomato Sauce (page 70)
¼ teaspoon chopped tarragon
¼ teaspoon chopped parsley

Cut stems from mushrooms level with the caps. Clean and dry them and cut in thin slices. Melt butter in a saucepan, add mushrooms, salt and pepper and cook, shaking the pan frequently, until the mushrooms are golden. Add shallots and wine and cook until reduced to about one half the original quantity. Add Brown and Tomato Sauces, tarragon and parsley. Used for meat and poultry.

DEVIL (DIABLE) SAUCE

2 tablespoons finely chopped
*   shallots*
8 crushed peppercorns
1 glass (3 ounces) white wine
*   (or vinegar)*

1 cup Brown Sauce
*   (page 68)*
1 teaspoon Worcestershire
*   Sauce*
¼ teaspoon chopped parsley

Put shallots and wine in a saucepan and cook until reduced to a thick paste. Add Brown Sauce and Worcestershire Sauce and strain. Add parsley. Used for grilled foods.

FINES HERBES SAUCE

3 sprigs tarragon
3 sprigs chervil
1 teaspoon chopped chives
3 sprigs chopped parsley

1 glass (3 ounces) white wine
2 tablespoons butter
1 teaspoon chopped shallots
1 cup Brown Sauce (page 68)

1 lemon

Remove and chop the stems of tarragon and chervil (saving the leaves to finish the sauce). Put the chopped stems with chives, parsley and wine in a saucepan, bring to a boil. Remove from heat and let stand about 10 minutes to make an infusion. In another saucepan, melt 1 tablespoon of butter, add shallots and the strained infusion. Cook until reduced to about one half the original quantity. Add Brown Sauce and cook 10 to 15 minutes. Add the juice of the lemon. Add remaining tablespoon of butter, swirling it into the sauce by moving the pan in a circular motion. Do not boil sauce after adding butter. When it has just melted, add the chopped leaves of tarragon and chervil. Used for meat, poultry and eggs.

GENEVOISE SAUCE (for Salmon)

1 carrot
1 onion
A little thyme
A small bay leaf
3 to 4 sprigs parsley
1 tablespoon butter

Trimmings, bones, chopped head, etc, of a salmon (or Dover sole)
1 pint red wine
1 cup Brown Sauce (page 68) (or 1 tablespoon butter and 1 teaspoon flour)

Make a Bordelaise mirepoix as follows: cut carrot and onion into very fine dice and put in a saucepan with thyme, bay leaf, parsley and butter. Cook very slowly for 15 to 20 minutes shaking the pan occasionally to prevent scorching. To the mirepoix add the trimmings, bones, head, etc, of the fish, mix all together and cook for

5 minutes more. Add wine and cook until reduced to about three fourths the original quantity. Add Brown Sauce. (If Brown Sauce is not available, cream the butter and flour together and add it to the saucepan just before the wine, mixing it in well with the other ingredients.) Bring back to the boil, strain and correct the seasoning with salt. Used for salmon, salmon trout or other fish.

ITALIENNE SAUCE

1 teaspoon chopped shallots
2 tomatoes, peeled, seeded and chopped
¾ cup Marsala wine
½ cup Brown Sauce (page 68) or Tomato Sauce (page 70)

2 tablespoons Mushroom Duxelles (page 32)
2 tablespoons chopped cooked ham
1 teaspoon chopped parsley

Put shallots, tomatoes and wine in a saucepan and cook until tomatoes are soft and mixture has reduced to about one half the original quantity. Add Brown (or Tomato) Sauce, Mushroom Duxelles and ham. Bring to a boil and cook about 5 minutes. Add parsley. Used for meat, fish or poultry. An especially good sauce for leftover meat.

LYONNAISE SAUCE

2 tablespoons butter
2 finely chopped onions
1 glass (3 ounces) white wine (or 2 tablespoons vinegar)

1 cup Brown Sauce (page 68)
1 teaspoon chopped parsley

Melt butter in a saucepan, add onions and cook until golden brown. Add wine and cook until reduced to about one half the original quantity (or add vinegar). Add Brown Sauce and cook slowly 15 minutes. Add parsley. Used for meat, especially leftover meat like boiled beef, and for vegetables such as artichoke bottoms.

MADEIRA SAUCE

2 cups Demi-glacé or Espagnole (page 69)   1 glass (3 ounces) Madeira

Cook Demi-glacé or Espagnole until reduced to about 1 cup and add Madeira. Bring back to a boil but do not allow to boil as this will cause the fine flavour of the wine to disappear. Used for beef, veal, ham or poultry.

MUSHROOM MADEIRA SAUCE

1 pound mushrooms
2 tablespoons butter
¼ teaspoon salt
A little pepper
1 teaspoon finely chopped
  shallot

1 glass (3 ounces) Madeira
  (or dry Sherry)
1 cup Brown Sauce
  (page 68)
½ teaspoon chopped
  parsley

Cut stems from mushrooms level with the caps. Clean and dry caps and cut in thick slices. (If mushrooms are very small leave whole.) Melt butter in a saucepan, add mushrooms, salt, pepper and cook, shaking the pan frequently, until mushrooms are golden. Add shallot, Madeira (or Sherry) and Brown Sauce. Bring to a boil and cook slowly 5 to 8 minutes and add chopped parsley. Used for meat, especially filet mignon, and for poultry.

MADEIRA SAUCE (for Sauteed Meat)

1 glass (3 ounces) Madeira or
  dry Sherry
1 cup Brown Sauce (page 68)
  2 tablespoons Madeira

1 teaspoon beef extract (or glacé-
  de-viande), if available
1 to 2 tablespoons butter

After the meat (filet mignon, escalope of veal or chicken) has been sautéed remove it from the pan and make the sauce right in the same pan. Pour off the fat but do not wash pan. Add the glass of Madeira or Sherry and cook, stirring in all the browned meat juices that cling to the pan, until the wine is reduced to about one half the original quantity. Add Brown Sauce and if it is available beef extract (or glacé-de-viande). Cook 5 to 10 minutes and add butter, swirling it in by moving the pan in a circular motion. Do not let sauce boil after adding butter. As soon as it is melted add remaining 2 tablespoons Madeira, swirling it in in the same way.

MUSTARD SAUCE (for Steaks and Chops)

½ teaspoonful English mustard	¼ teaspoon salt
2 tablespoons Worcestershire Sauce	A little pepper
	2 teaspoons lemon juice
½ cup Devil Sauce (page 74)	¼ cup heavy cream

Put all ingredients except the cream in a saucepan and cook slowly 10 minutes. Add cream and bring back to a boil. This sauce can be made up without the cream and kept in a covered jar in the refrigerator for several weeks. When ready to serve it, bring to a boil, add cream and bring back to the boil. Used for steaks and chops.

PERIGUEUX SAUCE

Madeira Sauce (page 77)	A little truffle liquor
1 tablespoon chopped truffles	1 tablespoon butter

Make Madeira Sauce and add truffles and truffle liquor to it. Add butter swirling it in by moving the pan in a circular motion until butter is melted. Do not let sauce boil after butter is added. Used for croquettes, for baked eggs, eggs *en cocotte* and for chicken.

PERIGOURDINE SAUCE

Follow recipe for périgueux sauce (above) using truffles cut in ¼-inch dice instead of chopped ones. Used for feathered game like pheasant, guinea hen, partridge or for poultry.

PORTUGAISE SAUCE

2 tablespoons butter
1 teaspoon finely chopped shallot
½ glass (2 ounces) red or white wine
2 tomatoes, peeled, seeded and chopped

½ cup Brown Sauce (page 68)
½ cup Tomato Sauce (page 70) (or tomato purée)
1 teaspoon chopped parsley
¼ teaspoon salt
A little pepper

Melt butter in a saucepan, add shallot and wine. Cook until reduced to one third the original quantity. Add tomatoes and cook until they are soft. Add Brown and Tomato Sauces, parsley, salt and pepper. Bring to the boil. Used for any meat or poultry.

PIQUANTE SAUCE Number I

1 tablespoon butter
1 finely chopped onion
2 tablespoons vinegar
1 cup Brown Sauce (page 68)

1 tablespoon Tomato Sauce (page 70) (or tomato purée)
3 tablespoons finely chopped sour pickles

1 teaspoon chopped parsley

Melt butter in a saucepan, add onion and cook until onion is lightly browned. Add vinegar and cook until reduced to almost nothing. Add Brown Sauce, Tomato Sauce (or tomato purée) and cook about 10 minutes. Add pickles and parsley. Correct the seasoning with salt. Used for fresh ox or veal tongue or any mild-flavoured meat and for reheating leftover meat. If Brown Sauce is not available, make Piquante Sauce Number II.

PIQUANTE SAUCE Number II

1 finely chopped onion
⅛ cup vinegar
1¼ cups strained, canned tomatoes
⅛ teaspoon salt
A little pepper

1 teaspoon flour
2 tablespoons butter
3 tablespoons finely chopped
  sour pickles
1 teaspoon chopped parsley

Put onion and vinegar in a saucepan and cook slowly until reduced to almost nothing. Add tomatoes, salt and pepper and cook slowly about 10 minutes. Cream together flour and butter and add, stirring it in until butter is melted and sauce thickened. Add pickles and parsley.

ROSSINI SAUCE

Follow recipe for Perigueux Sauce (page 78) using sliced truffles instead of chopped ones. Used with Tournedos of beef, breast of chicken, sweetbreads and foie gras.

ROUENNAISE SAUCE Number I

1 tablespoon butter
1 teaspoon chopped shallots
1 glass (3 ounces) red wine
⅛ cup Brown Sauce

3 to 4 chopped duck or chicken
  livers
Salt
Pepper

Melt butter in a saucepan, add shallots and cook until soft but not brown. Add wine and cook until reduced to almost nothing. Add Brown Sauce. When ready to serve, add the livers and rub through a fine sieve. Return to the fire to thicken, stirring constantly, but do not allow to boil. Correct the seasoning with salt and pepper. Used for duck, either domestic or wild. See also Rouennaise Sauce Number II, pages 128–9.

ROBERT SAUCE

1 tablespoon butter
2 tablespoons finely chopped
   onions
1 glass (3 ounces) white wine
1 tablespoon vinegar
1 cup Brown Sauce (page 68)

2 tablespoons Tomato Sauce
   (page 70) (or tomato purée)
1 teaspoon prepared mustard
1 tablespoon finely chopped
   sour pickles
1 teaspoon chopped parsley

Melt butter in a saucepan, add onions and cook until they are golden brown. Add wine and vinegar and cook until reduced to three fourths the original quantity. Add Brown and Tomato Sauces and cook slowly 10 to 15 minutes. When ready to serve, add mustard, pickles and chopped parsley. Used for pork, pork chops and leftover meat.

ROMAINE SAUCE

2 tablespoons sugar
½ cup vinegar
1 cup Brown Sauce (page 68)

2 tablespoons dry raisins
   (Smyrna or Corinth preferred)

Put sugar in heavy saucepan and cook until melted and a light golden colour. Add vinegar and cook until reduced to almost nothing. Add Brown Sauce, bring to the boil and add raisins. Cook slowly 8 to 10 minutes longer. Used for veal, beef, tongue and venison.

TORTUE SAUCE

1 glass (3 ounces) Madeira or dry Sherry
1 teaspoon herbs-à-tortue (mixed dried marjoram, rosemary, sage, bayleaf, thyme and basil)
1 cup boiling Brown Sauce (page 68)

Bring the wine to a boil and add the herbs. Let infuse 5 to 10 minutes and strain through cheesecloth. Add to the Brown Sauce. Used for turtle or for calf's head.

TOURANGELLE (RED-WINE) SAUCE

2 tablespoons butter	2 glasses (8 ounces) red wine
1 chopped carrot	2 cups stock or water
1 chopped onion	2 sprigs parsley
2 teaspoons chopped shallot	A little thyme
1 clove crushed garlic	1 small bay leaf
Bones of chicken or veal (if on hand)	1 teaspoon salt
	6 peppercorns
¼ cup flour	Mushroom peelings (if on hand)

Melt butter in a saucepan, add onion and carrot and cook until they start to turn golden. Add shallots, garlic, bones and flour. Mix all together well and cook until flour is golden brown. Add remaining ingredients, bring to the boil, stirring constantly. Cook slowly, stirring occasionally and skimming as needed, 1 to 1¼ hours. Strain through a fine sieve, bring back to the boil and correct the seasoning with salt. Used for any meat, leftover meat or for poached eggs. This sauce may be kept in a covered jar in the refrigerator for several days.

The following recipes are examples of dishes sauced the French way with Brown Sauces.

BEEF au GRATIN

2 tablespoons butter	Salt and pepper
3 medium onions, chopped	2 teaspoons vinegar
1 tablespoon flour	2 or 3 sour pickles, sliced
1 cup stock	1 teaspoon chopped parsley
¼ cup bread crumbs	

½ cup canned tomatoes or tomato juice
1 pound leftover cooked beef cut in slices

Melt butter in saucepan, add onions and cook slowly until golden. Add flour and cook a few minutes longer. Add stock and tomatoes, salt and pepper and cook, stirring until it comes to a boil. Continue cooking slowly 20 to 25 minutes, stirring occasionally. Add vinegar, sliced pickles and parsley. Do not let boil after adding pickles. (For a sharper sauce, add ½ teaspoon dry mustard mixed with 2 teaspoons vinegar or 1 teaspoon grated horseradish.) Arrange slices of meat in a heat-proof serving dish. Pour sauce over meat and keep hot until ready to serve. Then sprinkle with bread crumbs and brown in a hot oven or under grill. Do not let the sauce boil. Serves four or five.

CHICKEN en CASSEROLE (with Tarragon)

3 to 3½ pound chicken   2 tablespoons butter
4 to 5 stalks tarragon   ½ teaspoon salt
            ½ cup water

Clean and singe chicken. Remove leaves from tarragon for the garnish and put the 2 or 3 stalks in cavity of chicken. Sprinkle salt in cavity and on outside of chicken. Truss for roasting and place on side in roasting pan. Spread top with butter. Add water to pan. Cook in a moderately hot oven of 400 to 425 degrees, uncovered, 20 to 25 minutes, turn and cook on other side 20 to 25 minutes. When it is a good brown all over turn occasionally, basting often with the butter skimmed from the juice in the pan. If water cooks away add a little more. Put chicken on its back for the last few minutes to brown the breast. When chicken is done no pink juice will follow the fork which is withdrawn from the second joint to test it, it will be clear and colourless. Remove from pan, letting juice run from cavity into the pan, and place on serving dish. Chop the remaining branches of tarragon and add to pan, add a little water to make about ½ cup sauce, bring to a boil, correct the seasoning with salt and strain. Parboil the tarragon leaves a few minutes, dry well and use to decorate the chicken. Pour sauce over or serve separately.

MINUTE-STEAK SAUTE

2 tender thin steaks	1 to 2 tablespoons butter
Salt	1 glass (4 to 5 ounces) red or
A little pepper	white wine (or Sherry)

Season steaks with salt and pepper. Melt butter in shallow pan and when hot put in the steaks. Cook a few minutes on each side, 1 minute on each side for under-done, a little longer for medium and about 3 to 4 minutes on each side for well done. Remove from pan to hot dish. Add wine to pan and cook quickly to reduce a little, stirring in all the crustiness of the juice cooked on the pan and pour over the steaks.

MINUTE STEAK (with Shallot Sauce)

Follow recipe for Minute-Steak Sauté (above), adding 1 teaspoon finely chopped shallots (or onion) and ¼ teaspoon flour to butter in pan after removing steaks. Cook 1 minute (do not brown) and add wine. Cook as in Minute-Steak Sauté recipe. Serve with 1 teaspoon chopped parsley sprinkled over the top.

SCALLOPINE OF VEAL PORTUGAISE

1¼ pounds veal	1 glass (4 ounces) white wine
Salt and pepper	3 or 4 fresh tomatoes, peeled,
Flour	seeded and cut in quarters
3 tablespoons butter	¼ cup tomato juice
1 teaspoon chopped shallot or	¼ teaspoon flour
chopped onion	1 teaspoon chopped parsley

Have veal cut in very thin slices from the loin or any tender part and have butcher pound them with a mallet to make very thin. Season with salt and pepper and rub with flour. Melt 2 tablespoons butter in a saucepan. When it is very hot, put in the veal, a few slices at a time and cook until golden brown, about 3 or 4 minutes on each side. Remove meat to a serving dish. Add shallot or onion to saucepan. Add wine and cook until reduced to about half the original quantity. Add tomatoes and tomato juice. Cook about 15 minutes or until tomatoes are cooked and mixture is reduced to half the original quantity. Thicken the sauce with Manie Butter, made by creaming together the remaining tablespoon butter and ½ teaspoon flour. When the Manie Butter is blended into the sauce, add the chopped parsley and pour sauce over the meat. Serves four to five.

VEAL-KIDNEY STEW

4 veal kidneys	1 onion, minced
½ teaspoon salt	1 tablespoon flour
A little pepper	½ glass white wine (optional)
2 tablespoons butter	1 cup canned tomatoes
2 tablespoons veal-kidney fat	½ teaspoon chopped parsley

Mince kidneys and season with salt and pepper. Melt veal fat and let become very hot in a saucepan. Add kidneys and cook for 5 to 7 minutes, then remove them and put in a colander to drain. Discard all fat from pan. Put butter in pan with onion and when onion is golden brown add flour and mix all together. Add wine (if used), tomatoes and parsley and cook all together until sauce has thickened. Add kidneys and cook until they have reheated but do not allow the mixture to boil after the kidneys are in it. Serves four.

VEAL-KIDNEY STEW

IV. BUTTER SAUCES

IV. BUTTER SAUCES

BUTTER is a most important ingredient in all French cooking, so the simple Butter Sauces, although not great in number and relatively easy to make, occupy their own special place in the cuisine. They add a really tasty finish to a dish in about as quick and easy a way as any I know. They can be divided most conveniently in two groups. One group includes those that are made by creaming or browning the butter and serving it plain or with the addition of parsley, lemon juice and bread crumbs, such sauces as Meunière Butter, Maître d'Hôtel Butter, Polonaise Sauce and a few others. The other group consists of *les beurres composés*, or compounded butters, the combinations of butter with other highly flavoured ingredients such as shellfish, mustard, tarragon, shallots, wine and so on.

The Butter Sauces are usually served with grilled or fried fish and meat and some of them are particularly nice on such vegetables as cauliflower and broccoli. The compounded butters, especially the fish butters, have another use that is very popular and that is for canapés and other appetizers and also for small sandwiches that are made for hors d'oeuvres and tea trays. These highly flavoured butters are spread on biscuits, bread or toast or they are supplemented with other complementary flavours like a little mustard or some chopped chives.

The following pointers will prove helpful in making Butter Sauces.

... The butter in Butter Sauces should not be melted to the point of oiliness unless the recipe definitely specifies it (as in the case of Meunière Butter) but merely brought to a creamy consistency. Final melting should take place on the hot food.

... In making Black Butter cook it slowly to insure a more even brown colour and a better flavour.

... If the fish butters that require a pink colour such as Lobster or Crawfish Butter are too pale, add a very little pink vegetable colouring.

... In making Butter Sauces allow about one tablespoon butter for each serving. The four simple basic Butter Sauces are Brown, Black, Meunière and Maître d'Hôtel. They are the simplest of all sauces to make, yet are delicious and the most appropriate accompaniment for many foods.

BROWN BUTTER

Use about 1 tablespoon of butter for each serving. Put in saucepan, melt and then cook slowly until it is hazelnut brown. Used for vegetables such as asparagus and broccoli and for brains.

BLACK BUTTER

Continue cooking Brown Butter (above) until it is a very dark brown, almost black. It must be cooked very slowly to insure an even colour and a good flavour. Used for fish, vegetables and brains.

MEUNIERE BUTTER

Add a little lemon juice and a little chopped parsley to Brown Butter. Used for fish.

MAITRE d'HOTEL BUTTER

½ cup butter	½ lemon
1 teaspoon chopped parsley	Salt
	Pepper

Cream butter and add parsley, the juice of the lemon and salt and pepper to taste. Used for grilled fish and for grilled meats.

There are four important fish butters which are used in serving fish. Anchovy Butter is spread on the cooked fish but the other three, Crawfish, Lobster and Shrimp Butters are used for flavouring sauces made to serve with the fish.

ANCHOVY BUTTER

6 tablespoons butter
2 tablespoons anchovy paste (or well-pounded fillets of anchovy)

Cream butter, add anchovy paste and combine well. Used for baked or grilled fish.

CRAWFISH BUTTER

1 finely chopped onion
1 finely chopped carrot
1 small bay leaf

A little thyme
12 to 15 crawfish carcasses
½ pound butter

Put onion, carrot, bay leaf and thyme in a saucepan with 1 table-spoon butter. Cook slowly a few minutes or until vegetables are soft. Chop or crush (or run through meat grinder) the crawfish carcasses and place on top of the vegetables. Cover pan and cook all together very slowly for 30 minutes. Cool, add remaining butter and pound all together well until butter is creamy. Rub through a fine sieve. Used for finishing Mornay Sauce to serve with fish.

LOBSTER BUTTER

1 cooked lobster shell (and
    coral if obtainable)

½ pound butter
2 tablespoons water

Crush or pound (or run through meat grinder) the lobster shell plus all the creamy part of the lobster that clings to it and the coral, if it is obtainable. Combine with butter and cream all together. Put in top of double boiler, add water and melt slowly. Strain through cheesecloth. Cool. When butter has become firm on top of the liquid, spoon it off. Used for finishing sauces to serve with fish.

SHRIMP BUTTER

12 to 15 cooked shrimps   *½ pound butter*

Crush or pound (or run through meat grinder) shrimps. Combine with butter and cream all together. When very creamy, strain through a fine sieve. Used for finishing sauces to serve with fish.

MANIE BUTTER (BEURRE MANIE)

A thickening agent for sauces rather than a real sauce. Cream together butter and flour in the proportion of about 1 tablespoon butter and 1 teaspoon flour. Add to the liquid, gravy, sauce or whatever is to be thickened and bring just to the boil but do not boil. The above proportion is used with 1 to 2 cups gravy or sauce, the amount depending, however, upon the other thickening agents (starchy ingredients or egg yolks) in the mixture and also upon the thickness desired in the finished sauce.

ALMOND BUTTER

½ cup almonds   *½ cup butter*

Blanch almonds in hot water and remove skins. Pound to a paste adding a little water if necessary. Gradually add the butter, creaming all together. Strain through a fine sieve. Used for sautéed chicken or other 'amandine' dishes; and also for some pastries.

BERCY BUTTER

2 teaspoons finely chopped   *4 tablespoons butter*
*   shallots*   *2 teaspoons chopped parsley*
1 glass (5 ounces) dry white wine   *Salt and pepper*

Cook shallots and wine together until reduced to about one fourth the original quantity. Cool. Cream butter with parsley and add to wine and shallot mixture. Season with salt and pepper. Used for grilled meats.

COLBERT BUTTER

1 teaspoon melted beef extract
(or glacé-de-viande or concentrated veal gravy)

1 teaspoon chopped tarragon
1 cup Maître d'Hôtel butter
(page 91)

Combine all ingredients. Used for fried fish.

GARLIC BUTTER

6 cloves garlic   6 tablespoons butter

Boil the garlic in a little water for 5 to 7 minutes. Drain, crush and pound well, mixing at the same time with the butter. Strain through a fine sieve. Garlic Butter can also be made by crushing some garlic very fine and mixing it with creamed butter. Used for fish and baked oysters.

GREEN BUTTER

1 tablespoon parsley
1 teaspoon chervil
1 teaspoon tarragon leaves

6 to 8 spinach leaves
2 chopped shallots
4 to 6 tablespoons butter

Parboil the first 5 ingredients in just enough water to cover for 5 minutes. Remove from heat and plunge into cold water, then drain and dry them well in a towel. Pound to a paste, mixing at the same time with the butter. Strain through a fine sieve. Used for finishing sauces to give a green colour; also used for grilled fish.

CARLTON BUTTER

6 tablespoons butter
1 teaspoon Worcestershire
Sauce

2 teaspoons finely chopped
chutney
2 teaspoons chili sauce

Cream butter and add remaining ingredients. Used for grilled fish.

MARCHAND de VIN BUTTER

2 teaspoons finely chopped
shallots
1 glass (5 ounces) red wine

4 tablespoons butter
1 teaspoon chopped parsley
Salt and pepper

Cook shallots and wine together until reduced to one fourth the original quantity. Cool. Cream butter and parsley together and combine with the shallot and wine mixture. Season with salt and pepper. Used for grilled meats.

MONTPELLIER BUTTER

1 cup chopped leaves of
watercress, tarragon, parsley,
chervil in equal amounts
1 cup chopped spinach leaves
2 finely chopped shallots
1 finely chopped sour pickle,
well drained
1 tablespoon capers

1 fillet of anchovy
1 clove garlic
2 mashed hard-boiled egg
yolks
1 cup butter
2 tablespoons salad oil
Salt
Pepper

Parboil all the leaves for a few minutes, drain and press to remove as much water as possible. Crush and pound them to make a sort of paste. Parboil shallots, drain and combine with sour pickle, capers, anchovy and garlic. Crush and pound this to a sort of paste.

Combine with the paste of the leaves. Add egg yolks. Cream the butter and mix all together. Add the oil and correct the seasonings with salt and pepper. Rub through a fine sieve. Should be a light-green colour. Used for grilled, fried and boiled fish.

POLONAISE SAUCE

¼ *pound butter*   2 *tablespoons fine dry bread crumbs*

Melt butter and continue cooking until it starts to turn brown. Add crumbs and continue cooking until they are golden brown. Used for vegetables like asparagus, broccoli and cauliflower. The correct way to use this sauce is to put finely chopped hard-boiled egg on the vegetable, then the Polonaise Sauce and finally a sprinkling of finely chopped parsley over all.

MUSTARD BUTTER

6 *tablespoons butter*   2 *teaspoons prepared mustard*

Melt butter and add the mustard little by little. Used for fish.

PAPRIKA BUTTER

6 *tablespoons butter*   2 *tablespoons chopped onion*
1 *teaspoon paprika*

Melt 2 tablespoons butter, add onion and cook until light brown. Add paprika, mix well and let cool. Cream remaining 4 tablespoons butter and add to first mixture. Strain through a fine sieve. Used for fish, baked oysters, escalope of veal and for finishing Paprika Sauce.

SHALLOT BUTTER

4 teaspoons finely chopped shallots
6 tablespoons butter

Finely chopped chives (if available)

Parboil shallots in a little water for 1 or 2 minutes. Drain and dry on a towel. Combine with butter, crushing all together well. Strain through a fine sieve. The addition of a little finely chopped chives is an improvement. Used for grilled meats.

TARRAGON BUTTER

6 tablespoons tarragon leaves   6 tablespoons butter

Parboil tarragon leaves in a little water for 2 or 3 minutes. Drain and dry on a towel. Combine with 6 tablespoons butter, crushing all together well. Strain through a fine sieve. Used for grilled meats and grilled fish.

BUTTER FOR SNAILS (Escargots)

¾ pound butter
2 teaspoons chopped shallots
4 cloves garlic, crushed to a
    fine paste

1 tablespoon chopped
    parsley
1 teaspoon salt
Pepper

Cream butter and combine with remaining ingredients, crushing all together well. Put snails back in the shells and fill each one up with the prepared butter. Dip in fresh bread crumbs, sprinkle with a little butter and bake in a hot oven until the butter is bubbling in the shells and they are brown on top. This amount is sufficient for 50 snails.

TOMATO BUTTER

4 ripe tomatoes   *4 tablespoons butter*

Peel, seed and chop tomatoes, put in a saucepan and cook until all surplus moisture is cooked away. Cool. Cream butter and combine with tomatoes. Strain through a fine sieve. Used for finishing Mornay Sauce and for certain poached-egg and fish recipes.

VIERGE BUTTER

6 tablespoons butter   *A little salt*
½ lemon   *A little white pepper*

Put all ingredients in the top of a double boiler and whip all together until butter becomes soft and fluffy. Used for asparagus or for other boiled vegetables.

WHITE BUTTER

1 glass (3 ounces) vinegar   *1 teaspoon chopped parsley*
1 teaspoon chopped shallots   *Salt*
4 tablespoons butter   *Pepper*

Cook vinegar and shallots together until reduced to one fourth the original quantity. Cool to lukewarm. Cream butter and combine with vinegar and shallot mixture. Add parsley and season with salt and pepper. Used for boiled fish, especially freshwater fish.

The following recipes are examples of dishes sauced the French way with Butter Sauces.

ASPARAGUS POLONAISE

Cook asparagus and drain well. Put coarsely chopped hard-cooked eggs on top of tips and sprinkle with chopped parsley. Cook fine fresh bread crumbs in butter until they are brown, then pour butter and crumbs over eggs, using 2 tablespoons crumbs and 4 tablespoons butter for each bunch of 18 to 24 asparagus stalks.

CALF'S LIVER ALBERT KELLER

4 slices calf's liver	*1 glass (4 ounces) Sherry*
Flour	*Few slices crisp bacon*
2 tablespoons butter	*Chopped parsley*
Chopped chives	

Rub liver with the flour. Melt butter in skillet. When hot, put in the slices of liver and cook about 2 or 3 minutes on each side until golden brown. (If wanted medium or well done, cook a little longer.) Remove liver to serving dish, add wine to saucepan and cook until reduced a little. Pour over liver. Garnish with bacon, sprinkle chopped parsley and chives over all.

FISH SAUTE MEUNIERE

Fish may be whole, in fillets or slices, according to size. Dip in milk and then in flour seasoned with salt and pepper. Put about $\frac{1}{4}$ inch of salad oil in a frying pan and heat very hot. Add fish and cook until golden brown on both sides. Remove to serving dish, sprinkle with a little pepper, a few drops of lemon juice, and a little chopped parsley. For each serving cook 1 tablespoon butter until it is hazelnut brown in colour and pour over the fish. Place a slice of peeled lemon on top.

SHAD-ROE AMANDINE

Dip shad roe in milk and sprinkle with flour. Put enough salad oil in frying pan to cover bottom of pan. Heat oil, but not too hot, and put in the roe. Cook slowly with the pan partly covered, turning roe when underside is brown. Cook until done, about 12 to 15 minutes, depending upon thickness. Shad roe is firm when done, but to be sure, make a little cut in the side of the piece with a sharp knife and if done the inside will not be red. Garnish with sliced almonds that have been browned in the oven and pour Brown Butter (page 91) over the roe.

V. COLD SAUCES

V. COLD SAUCES

THE Cold Sauces in general are quite simple to make but if you are able to make them well you have developed a good sense of flavour and a discretion with seasonings. The only sauce in this group that is difficult to make is Mayonnaise. Once it is mastered you have all the cold entrée sauces under control.

The Cold Sauces are used for appetizers, salads and also for cold and some hot entrées. They are piquant with the spiciness of herbs, pickles and mustard, tangy with the sharpness of vinegar or lemon juice. We think of them as the perfect accompaniment for cold foods and especially good with fish and shellfish. And mild foods that are bolstered with one of these piquant sauces become actually appetite provoking. Mayonnaise, however, is an exception to this piquancy characteristic. Its appeal lies in its smooth delicacy rather than in any pronounced flavour. But Mayonnaise, let no one forget, is one sauce that has really stood the test of time. Its popularity has never waned since the early 1600's when Cardinal Richelieu discovered this combination of oil and egg yolks which he flavoured with lemon juice. We still make Mayonnaise the same way today.

Cold Sauces are, of course, essential for the cold buffet. Most fine restaurants both here and abroad provide this type of service in summertime and some continue the custom during the winter, too, especially for luncheon. The buffet tables usually have twenty to thirty elaborately garnished cold dishes including hors d'oeuvres, cold cuts, meat, poultry, fish and shellfish dishes, foie gras and other pâtés and also many kinds of salads. Each dish is placed on a bed of ice laid in deep oblong silver trays. Any hostess with a large group to entertain will find this a most convenient way of serving a repast. The food can be prepared far ahead of serving time, which in itself is a great convenience, and little help is needed to serve it. At home parties the food is eaten within a relatively short time, not required to stand for hours as in a restaurant, and so ice is not necessary under the dishes of food. But Cold Sauces don't end with the cold buffet. Many luncheon and most dinner menus include either a cold appetizer or a salad and often both. Furthermore, many hot dishes are sauced with cold sauces, for example, fish with Tartare Sauce and calf's head or brains with Vinaigrette Sauce.

Mayonnaise is used with many foods and it is also the foundation for any number of other sauces which include such additional ingredients as pickles, chili sauce and other complementary flavours. Because its characteristic consistency depends upon egg yolks, Mayonnaise unfortunately has a tendency to separate and become a curdled mass instead of a smooth emulsion. But this need never happen if these four simple rules are always followed. One, have both egg yolks and oil at room temperature, never just out of the refrigerator. Two, don't try to combine more oil with the yolks than they can hold in emulsion – one cup of oil to two egg yolks is about right. Three, add the first spoonful of oil a few drops at a time and then continue in a thin stream like a thread, whipping the mixture constantly and adding a little of the vinegar whenever the mixture gets too thick. Four, don't store Mayonnaise in an automatic refrigerator because extreme cold will congeal the oil and cause separation. Mayonnaise is standard but its variations are far from standard. Different chefs, different cook books and even different localities put together combinations that vary as to the ingredients and the amounts of these ingredients to be added in making Tartare Sauce, Russian Dressing and other popular combinations. The recipes in this book are the formulas that I have used for many years.

The following pointers will prove helpful in achieving an interesting Cold-Sauce repertoire.

. . . In combining pickles or capers with Mayonnaise be sure to press out as much moisture as possible before adding them in order to avoid diluting the sauce.

. . . If a sharper dressing is desired do not increase the vinegar but instead add some mustard, either dry or prepared. The flavour will be better.

. . . If Mayonnaise should separate it can be brought back to a smooth emulsion by taking another egg yolk and gradually beating in the curdled mixture, starting with a teaspoon at a time and then gradually increasing the quantity of the additions.

. . . Mayonnaise should be stored in a cool place but not in the refrigerator unless it has a special compartment not as cold as the rest of the box.

. . . If lemon juice is substituted for vinegar in a Cold-Sauce recipe only one half or one third as much lemon juice should be used because its flavour is much stronger.

. . . The terms Vinaigrette Sauce and French Dressing are used interchangeably, but as a rule French Dressing is considered the simple mixture of oil, vinegar, salt and pepper with perhaps *fines herbes* and garlic. Vinaigrette Sauce usually implies the inclusion of chopped pickles, chopped hard-cooked eggs, mustard and other ingredients preferred with hors d'oeuvres.

MAYONNAISE

2 egg yolks
½ teaspoon salt
½ teaspoon dry (or prepared)
    mustard

A little pepper
1 teaspoon vinegar (or ½ tea-
    spoon lemon juice)
1 cup olive or salad oil

Rinse mixing bowl in hot water and dry thoroughly. Put in the egg yolks, salt, mustard, pepper and a few drops of vinegar and mix all together well. Add a few drops of the oil, beating vigorously and continue adding a few drops at a time until about 2 tablespoons have been added. Add a few drops of the vinegar. Add more oil in a thin stream, beating vigorously all the time. Add remaining vinegar as the mixture gets thick. If mayonnaise seems too thick a little water may be added instead of the remaining vinegar. Used for fish, meat, poultry, vegetable and fruit salads and for cold fish such as salmon.

LIGHT MAYONNAISE

1 cup Mayonnaise (above)
Juice of ½ lemon

2 tablespoons whipped
    cream

Combine Mayonnaise and lemon juice and fold in the whipped cream. Used for salads containing fruit.

MAYONNAISE à la MINT

Scald 2 tablespoons vinegar and pour over 2 teaspoons chopped mint leaves. Cool and strain. Use 1 tablespoon for the vinegar called for in Mayonnaise (above). Add a few chopped mint leaves to the finished Mayonnaise. Used for cold vegetables such as broccoli and for cold fish.

MAYONNAISE CHAUD FROID

2 tablespoons unflavoured
   gelatine

¼ cup cold water
2 cups Mayonnaise (ab

Soften gelatine in cold water, set bowl over hot water and steam until gelatine is thoroughly dissolved. Fold into Mayonnaise, mixing all together well. Use for coating fish or lobster on which decorations are to be arranged.

FRENCH DRESSING
or VINAIGRETTE SAUCE

1 tablespoon vinegar
3 to 4 tablespoons olive or salad oil
¼ teaspoon salt

A little pepper
¼ teaspoon dry (or prepared) mustard (optional)

Mix all together well. The amount of oil depends upon the individual taste, also upon the strength of the vinegar. Used for tossed green salads, for hors d'oeuvres and for marinating salad mixtures.

VINAIGRETTE with FINES HERBES

1 tablespoon vinegar
3 to 4 tablespoons olive or
   salad oil
¼ teaspoon salt

¼ teaspoon dry (or prepared) mustard
1 teaspoon mixed, chopped parsley, tarragon, chervil and chives

Mix all together well. Used for tossed green salads, for hors d'oeuvres and for cold fish.

VINAIGRETTE for CALF'S FEET, BRAINS or HEAD

½ a cooked calf's brain   ½ cup Vinaigrette Sauce

Drain the calf's brain (that has been cooked in Court Bouillon) and crush with a fork. Combine with the Vinaigrette to thicken it. Used for calf's feet, brains or head.

VINAIGRETTE with MUSTARD

1 teaspoon prepared mustard
A little salt
A little pepper

1 teaspoon lemon juice (or 1 tablespoon vinegar)
4 tablespoons olive or salad oil

Mix together mustard, salt, pepper and lemon juice. Add oil, little by little, stirring vigorously until well combined. Used for cold fish, meats and vegetables and for combinations of them.

VINAIGRETTE for HORS d'ŒUVRES

2 tablespoons vinegar
3 tablespoons olive or salad oil
¼ teaspoon salt
A little pepper
1 teaspoon capers

1 teaspoon each chopped parsley, tarragon, chervil and chives
1 tablespoon chopped hard-boiled egg

Mix all together and combine well. Used for hors d'oeuvres.

AIOLI SAUCE

6 to 8 cloves of garlic   1 cup olive or salad oil

| ¼ teaspoon salt | ¼ cup mashed potato (optional) |
| 2 egg yolks | Juice of ¼ lemon |

Crush the garlic very thoroughly and combine with salt and egg yolks. Add oil a few drops at a time, beating vigorously until about 2 tablespoons have been added. Continue adding in a thin stream beating thoroughly all the time. If mixture seems to be too thick add a half teaspoon or more of water. (The mashed potato, either cold or lukewarm, is sometimes added at this point with the idea of preventing the sauce from separating.) Add the juice of the lemon. Used for hot or cold fish.

COCKTAIL SAUCE for SHELLFISH

1 cup tomato catsup	1 teaspoon horseradish
¼ cup chili sauce	Juice of 1 lemon
1 tablespoon vinegar	¼ teaspoon celery salt
1 teaspoon Worcestershire sauce	5 drops Tobasco Sauce

Mix all ingredients together. Used for shrimp, lobster, crabmeat, oyster and fish cocktails. This is the famous Ritz cocktail sauce.

CREAM MUSTARD

| 1 teaspoon prepared mustard | Few drops of lemon juice |
| A little salt | ½ cup heavy cream |

Add mustard, salt and lemon juice to cream which may be plain or may be whipped if a lighter sauce is desired. Used for chicken, fish and shellfish.

GREEN SAUCE

| 15 leaves watercress | 8 sprigs parsley |
| 15 leaves spinach | 2 cups Mayonnaise (page 106) |

Wash the watercress and spinach leaves and parsley thoroughly and cover with boiling water. Let stand 5 to 6 minutes. Drain, put in cold water and drain again pressing out all the surplus moisture. Rub the wilted greens through a fine strainer and combine with Mayonnaise, mixing all together well. Add more seasoning if desired. Used for cold salmon, lobster or other fish.

GRIBICHE SAUCE

3 hard-boiled eggs
½ teaspoon salt
1 teaspoon mustard
A little pepper
1½ cups olive or salad oil

½ cup vinegar
½ cup chopped sour pickles
1 tablespoon mixed chopped parsley, chervil, tarragon and chives

Separate the eggs and put the yolks in a bowl. Crush them until they are very smooth and add salt, mustard and pepper. Add oil a few drops at a time, beating vigorously, until about 2 tablespoons have been added. Then add it in a thin stream, beating vigorously all the time, and adding the vinegar a little at a time whenever the mixture starts to become too thick. Press out all the moisture from the pickles, chop the egg whites and add to the sauce along with the parsley, chervil and chives. Used for calf's feet or brains, for cold boiled beef, for chicken, fish and shellfish, and for any meats in the hors-d'oeuvres tray.

MINT SAUCE

2 tablespoons finely chopped mint leaves
1 tablespoon powdered sugar

A little salt
A little pepper
½ cup wine vinegar
½ cup cold water

Put all ingredients into a saucepan and bring to a boil. Cool. Used for roast lamb.

LORENZO DRESSING

½ cup chili sauce
⅔ cup olive or salad oil
¼ cup vinegar

½ teaspoon salt
¼ teaspoon pepper
Finely chopped watercress leaves

Mix all together and combine well. Used for tossed green salads, for dressing hearts of lettuce or endive and for fancy mixed salads of vegetables, fish or fruit.

MONA LISA DRESSING

¼ teaspoon paprika
½ teaspoon horseradish

¼ teaspoon English mustard
½ cup Mayonnaise (page 106)

1 tablespoon very heavy cream

Add paprika, horseradish and mustard to Mayonnaise and fold in the cream. If a lighter dressing is desired, the cream may be whipped. Used for dressing hearts of lettuce or endive and for fancy mixed salads of vegetables or fish.

NIÇOISE SAUCE

½ cup tomato purée
1 finely chopped pepper
(red or green)

1 teaspoon mixed, chopped
tarragon and chives
2 cups Mayonnaise (page 106)

Cook tomato purée until reduced to the thickness of Mayonnaise, stirring constantly to prevent scorching. Chill. Combine with the pepper, tarragon and chives. Fold into the Mayonnaise and mix well. Used for cold fish and shellfish.

RAVIGOTE SAUCE

2 tablespoons vinegar	1 chopped hard-boiled egg
3 tablespoons olive or salad oil	1 teaspoon mixed chopped parsley, tarragon and chervil
1 tablespoon finely chopped onion	¼ teaspoon salt
1 tablespoon prepared mustard	A little pepper

Mix all together well. Used for leftover meat and fish.

REMOULADE SAUCE

¼ cup finely chopped sour pickles	1 tablespoon mixed chopped parsley, tarragon and chervil
2 tablespoons finely chopped capers	
1 tablespoon prepared mustard	2 cups Mayonnaise (page 106)

Press out all the moisture from the pickles and capers. Then add them along with the mustard, parsley, tarragon and chervil to the Mayonnaise, mixing all together well. Used for fried fish and for cold fish and shellfish.

SAUCE à la RITZ

1 tablespoon chili sauce	1 teaspoon mixed chopped chervil, parsley and chives
¼ teaspoon Worcestershire Sauce	
1 tomato, peeled, seeded and chopped	1 cup Mayonnaise (page 106)

Add all the other ingredients to the Mayonnaise and mix well. Used for lobster, crab and other shellfish salads and appetizers.

RUSSIAN DRESSING

3 tablespoons chili sauce
1 teaspoon finely chopped
   pimiento

1 teaspoon finely chopped
   chives
1 cup Mayonnaise (page 106)

Add all the other ingredients to Mayonnaise and mix well. Used for fish and shellfish and to dress hearts of lettuce.

RUSSIAN DRESSING (for Lobster)

Tomalley (i.e. the liver) and
   coral of 1 cooked lobster
1 tablespoon caviar
1 teaspoon prepared mustard

1 to 1½ cups Mayonnaise
   (page 106)
1 teaspoon mixed chopped
   chives and parsley

Mix together the tomalley and coral of the lobster, add caviar and rub through a fine sieve. Add mustard and combine with Mayonnaise. Add chives and parsley and mix all together well. Used for cold shellfish, especially lobster.

THOUSAND-ISLAND DRESSING

1 tablespoon chili sauce
¼ teaspoon Worcestershire Sauce
1 tomato, peeled, seeded and
   chopped

½ teaspoon chopped pimiento
½ teaspoon chopped chives
1 cup Mayonnaise
   (page 106)

Add all the other ingredients to the Mayonnaise and mix well. Used for fish and shellfish salads and appetizers.

TARTARE SAUCE

6 *finely chopped ripe olives*   *Remoulade Sauce*
1 *teaspoon chopped chives*   (*page 112*)

Add olives and chives to the amount of Remoulade Sauce given
in the recipe. Used for fried fish.

VINCENT SAUCE

Follow the recipe for Green Sauce, adding 15 leaves of sorrel to
the other greens called for. Used for fish, especially with fried fish
like whitebait, but also with cold lobster, salmon, and other fish.

BROWN CHAUD FROID SAUCE

2 *tablespoons unflavoured gelatine*   1 *cup stock*
¼ *cup cold water*   1 *glass* (*4 ounces*) *Madeira*
2 *cups Brown Sauce* (*page 68*)   (*or Sherry*)

Soften gelatine in cold water for 5 minutes. Combine Brown Sauce
and stock and bring to a boil. Add gelatine, and stir until dissolved. Add Madeira (or Sherry). Used before it congeals for coating cold dishes of dark meat like braised beef, duckling and game.

WHITE CHAUD FROID SAUCE

2 *tablespoons unflavoured*   2 *cups Velouté* (*page 41*) (*or*
  gelatine   *Supreme Sauce* (*page 43*)
¼ *cup cold water*   1 *cup heavy cream*
                        Salt

Soften gelatine in cold water for 5 minutes. Bring Velouté (or Supreme Sauce) to a boil. Add gelatine and stir until dissolved. Add cream. Correct the seasoning with salt. Strain through a fine sieve. Cool. Used before it congeals for coating a chicken or other meat which will be served cold.

The following recipes are examples of dishes sauced the French way with Cold Sauces.

SPRING SALAD

½ cup cooked asparagus tips cut in pieces
½ cup cooked French beans
½ cup sliced radishes
2 cooked (or canned) artichoke bottoms, sliced
2 chopped hard-boiled eggs

1 teaspoon fines herbes (chopped parsley, tarragon, chervil and chives)
½ cup Vinaigrette (or French Dressing) (page 107)
½ teaspoon mustard
¼ cup Mayonnaise (page 106)

Mix together all the vegetables and the *fines herbes*. Add the mustard to the Vinaigrette or French Dressing and combine with the vegetables. Let marinate for about an hour. Just before serving, add the Mayonnaise.

TOSSED GREEN SALAD
a la FRANCAISE

Separate the leaves, remove bruised ones, from desired salad greens, lettuce, endive, chicory, escarole, etc., and wash in a large quantity of water. Drain and dry thoroughly by shaking in a towel. Cut or tear large leaves into smaller pieces and chill until ready to use. Crush a tiny bit of garlic with a little salt in the bottom of a chilled salad bowl or rub the inside of the bowl with a cut piece of garlic. Put the greens into the bowl and add Vinaigrette or

French Dressing (page 91) allowing about 1 tablespoon for each serving. Toss just before serving with large fork and spoon until all the leaves are coated with the dressing and none of it remains in the bottom of the bowl.

CELERY with APPLE (for Hors d'Œuvres)

Make a fine julienne of celery, about 1½ cups, put in cold water (or ice water) for 35 to 40 minutes to crisp. Drain. Put in a bowl and add 1 sour apple peeled, cored and finely minced. Mix with Sauce Vinaigrette with Mustard (page 108), Cream Mustard (page 109) or prepared mustard.

CRABMEAT COCKTAIL

Serve cooked crabmeat on 2 leaves of lettuce on a bed of finely crushed ice with a small glass of Cocktail Sauce in the centre and a piece of lemon. Or serve already mixed with the sauce in a glass cocktail dish.

SHRIMP COCKTAIL

Follow directions for Crabmeat Cocktail substituting cooked shrimp for the crabmeat.

VI. GAME SAUCES

VI. GAME SAUCES

TOO much game, I am sure, is poorly cooked and that which is nicely cooked is too often poorly sauced. As a consequence people say they don't like game. Actually, they have probably never rolled a deliciously sauced mouthful of well-cooked game over the tongue. But merely taking some flour to thicken the juice in the roasting pan or the liquid of the stew is not what I mean by making a good game sauce. I mean savour, the blending of such flavours as wine, spices, herbs, onion, carrot, celery, stock and butter, perhaps currant jelly or cream or whatever best complements the meat. I also mean texture, the juiciness and succulence imparted by the sauce and so essential in preparing certain kinds of game. Unlike domesticated animals and poultry, the wild ones have no planned feeding that insures a good proportion of fat and the kind of meat tissue that is juicy. Game dishes, therefore, must rely upon sauces to supply this lack. At the same time the right sauce can point up the unusual flavour which is the special contribution of each kind of game.

Game has its own pungency, its so-called gaminess, that asks for piquancy in the sauce served with it. And most connoisseurs believe that perfection is reached when there is a harmonious combination of game and sauce which is obtained by carrying the flavour of the game into the sauce. There are various ways of accomplishing this. With wild duck, for example, the carcass (bones and all the meat except the breast meat) is pressed in a special device – *la presse* – to extract the blood which gives a special savour and also thickens the sauce to be served on the breast meat. With furred game the marinade of wine, herbs and spices in which the game is pickled before cooking inevitably picks up some of the game flavour and some of this marinade is frequently used in making the sauce. With feathered game, either roasted or braised, the sauce is enriched with the juices in the pan in which the bird was cooked and in which the sauce should always be made or finished.

It is desirable, although not always possible, to have some of the blood of game to thicken the sauce. In the case of deer it is seldom possible because usually there is too great a lapse of time between killing and hanging the animal and the cooking of it. But often the blood of a rabbit or hare can be saved, and if necessary it can be kept for a couple of days in the refrigerator without coagulating if mixed with a little vinegar. The purpose of the blood is to thicken and colour the sauce and at the same time it adds a special flavour, too. You must remember, though, that in thickening a sauce with blood you cannot add it until the very last minute before serving, that the pan must be removed from the heat when adding the blood and that the sauce must never be boiled after the blood is added. Unless these rules are followed the sauce will curdle.

Poivrade Sauce is the most important of the game sauces. It is the traditional sauce to serve with venison and it is a basic sauce used in making many game sauces. Bread Sauce for grouse, and special Cream Sauces for both furred and feathered game are also traditional. There are times, however, when a game dish must be cooked and served more hurriedly than we know is desirable and then the best solution is to make one of the 'quick' sauces that are made in the pan after the game has finished cooking.

The following pointers will prove helpful in saucing the game that comes into the kitchen to be cooked.

... If no Brown Sauce is available for making Poivrade Sauce it is possible to make a brown roux and then use brown stock for the liquid in the sauce.

... When blood is called for in a game sauce recipe and none is available, you can substitute arrowroot or cornflour mixed with red wine, using one teaspoon of arrowroot for one half cup of wine.

... If it is necessary to keep blood for a sauce for a day or two, store it in the refrigerator but always mix it with vinegar, using one tablespoon vinegar for one half cup of blood.

... Peppercorns are important in most game sauces but should not be cooked too long in a sauce because then they impart a bitter flavour.

POIVRADE SAUCE Number I

5 tablespoons salad oil
1 sliced carrot
1 diced onion
3 to 4 sprigs parsley
1 bay leaf
A little thyme
¼ cup vinegar

¼ cup liquor from uncooked marinade (page 32)
10 peppercorns
1 glass (4 ounces) red wine
3 cups Brown Sauce (page 68)
Bones from game (if available)

Put oil in a saucepan, add carrot and onion and cook until golden brown. Add parsley, bay leaf, thyme, vinegar and ¼ cup of the marinade liquor. Cook until reduced to one third the original quantity and add Brown Sauce. If bones from the game are available put them in a flat pan and place in a hot oven and cook until they are brown while the sauce is cooking. Add them to the sauce at the same time the Brown Sauce is added, bring to a boil and cook slowly about 1 hour. Add peppercorns and cook a few minutes longer. Strain sauce into another pan and add the remaining ¼ cup of marinade liquor. Bring to a boil and cook slowly another 30 minutes skimming carefully all the time as the fat rises. Add wine. Correct the seasoning with salt and freshly ground pepper to make a hot sauce. This makes 3 cups of sauce. Used for all large furred game and also for saddle of hare and can also be used for a marinated leg of lamb or mutton. If no Brown Sauce is available, make the following Poivrade Sauce.

POIVRADE SAUCE Number II

6 tablespoons salad oil
1 sliced carrot
1 diced onion
½ cup flour
4 cups brown stock (page 30)
1 cup tomato purée (or juice)

A little thyme
Bones of game (if available)
½ cup vinegar
½ cup liquor from uncooked marinade (page 32)

3 to 4 sprigs parsley   6 peppercorns
1 bay leaf   1 glass (4 ounces) red wine

Put salad oil in a saucepan, add carrot and onion and cook until
they are golden. Add flour, mix all together and cook until the
flour turns golden brown. Add stock and tomato purée (or juice),
mix well with a whip and cook stirring until well blended. Add
parsley, bay leaf and thyme. If bones of game are available, spread
them in a shallow pan and brown them in a hot oven and add to
the sauce. Cook 1½ hours stirring occasionally and skimming as
needed. Put vinegar, liquor from the marinade and peppercorns
in another pan and cook until reduced to about one third the
original quantity. Strain the sauce into the reduced vinegar mixture and cook about 30 minutes longer, skimming carefully all the
time as the fat rises. Add wine. Correct the seasoning with salt
and add freshly ground pepper to make a hot sauce.

BIGARADE SAUCE

½ cup veal stock (or water)   Juice of 1 orange
½ teaspoon arrowroot (or cornflour)   Few drops lemon juice
1 tablespoon sugar   1 tablespoon Curaçao (or
1 tablespoon vinegar   Cointreau)
1 tablespoon fine julienne of orange rind Sections of orange

When duck is done remove from roasting pan and pour off all the
fat from the pan. Add veal stock or water and cook a few minutes,
stirring in all the browned juices clinging to the pan. Mix arrowroot (or cornflour) with a little water and add. In another pan mix
the sugar and vinegar and cook until reduced to a light brown
caramel. Strain the sauce from the roasting pan into the caramel-
ized sugar and vinegar and cook 5 minutes. Cook the julienne of
orange rind in water 5 minutes to remove any bitter flavour, drain
and add to the sauce. Add orange and lemon juice, correct the
seasoning with salt and add Curaçao (or Cointreau). Used for wild
or domestic duck, garnishing the dish with sections of orange.

BREAD SAUCE

1 *onion studded with*	*A little cayenne pepper*
2 *cloves*	*A little salt*
2 *cups milk*	1 *cup fresh bread crumbs*

Put onion and milk in a saucepan, add cayenne pepper and salt and bring to a boil. Cook 5 minutes, strain and add the bread crumbs. Correct the seasoning with salt. For a richer sauce finish with a little butter or cream. Used for roast wild birds and always with grouse.

CHEVREUIL SAUCE

1½ *cups Poivrade Sauce* (*page 122*)	½ *cup liquor from uncooked marinade* (*page 32*)
½ *cup red wine*	1 *teaspoon sugar*
2 *tablespoons butter*	

Bring Poivrade Sauce to a boil, add wine and liquor from the marinade. Cook 30 to 40 minutes skimming as necessary. Add sugar and cook until reduced to about 1¼ cups. Add butter swirling it in by moving the pan around in a circular motion. Do not cook after butter has melted. Strain. Used for venison or marinated leg of lamb or mutton.

CREAM SAUCE for VENISON or HARE

1 *tablespoon vinegar*	2 *tablespoons Cream Sauce* (*page 40*) (*or Velouté*) (*page 41*)
1 *cup heavy cream*	
2 *tablespoons Poivrade Sauce* (*page 122*)	*Salt*

When venison is cooked, remove from pan and pour off all the fat from the pan. Add vinegar and cream. Cook a few minutes or until reduced to about two thirds the original quantity. Add Poivrade Sauce and Cream Sauce (or Velouté). Correct the seasoning with salt. If the flavour of lemon juice is preferred to vinegar, omit vinegar and add 1 teaspoon lemon juice after the sauce is cooked. Used for roast or sautéed venison or roast saddle of hare.

CUMBERLAND SAUCE

3 finely chopped shallots
1 orange
1 lemon
A little powdered sugar
A little cayenne pepper

6 tablespoons melted currant
   jelly
5 tablespoons Port wine
½ teaspoon prepared mustard
   (optional)

Parboil shallots in water 1 or 2 minutes. Drain. Remove the zest – that is the thinnest peeling possible – of the surface skin of the orange and lemon, cut in fine julienne and parboil in water for 10 minutes. Drain well. Put shallots, orange and lemon rind in a bowl, add the juice of the orange and juice of one half the lemon and all the remaining ingredients. Add mustard if a sharper sauce is desired. Used for cold venison or other furred game or for any cold meat.

DIANE SAUCE

1 cup Poivrade Sauce
   (page 122)
1 cup whipped cream

1 to 2 truffles cut in julienne
1 hard-boiled egg,
   chopped

Add whipped cream to the Poivrade Sauce just before serving. Fold in the truffles (using one or two according to the size) and egg. Used for furred game.

GRAND VENEUR SAUCE

Add 2 tablespoons truffles cut in fine julienne or fine dice to 2 cups boiling Poivrade Sauce. If the blood of hare or rabbit is available thicken the sauce with it, adding it very slowly to the sauce, moving the pan in a circular motion to swirl it into the mixture. Do not cook the sauce after the blood has been added. Used for all large furred game.

DANOISE SAUCE

Add 1 tablespoon red currant jelly and 1 tablespoon of cooked ham cut in very small dice to Suedoise Sauce (Cream Sauce for Wild Birds) (page 129). Used for all wild birds.

MOSCOVITE SAUCE

2 cups Poivrade Sauce (page 122)
1 glass Madeira or Malaga wine
2 tablespoons almonds

1½ tablespoons raisins (Smyrna or Corinth preferred)

Bring Poivrade Sauce to a boil and cook 10 minutes. Remove from heat and add wine. Blanch the almonds, cut in slivers and toast. Parboil the raisins in a little water for a few minutes and drain or sauté them in a little butter. Add almonds and raisins to the sauce. Used for venison and other large furred game.

QUICK CREAM SAUCE for FURRED or FEATHERED GAME

2 teaspoons finely chopped shallots

½ cup strained liquor from uncooked marinade (if available)

2 tablespoons butter　　　1½ cups heavy cream
1½ teaspoons flour　　　　2 teaspoons currant jelly (optional)
　　　　　　Salt and pepper

Remove game from pan and pour off the fat from the pan. Put
shallots, butter and flour into roasting pan, mix all together and
cook about 2 minutes. Add the liquor from the uncooked marinade (if any is available) and blend all together. Add cream, stirring
it in slowly and cooking until the sauce is blended and thickened.
Add currant jelly if desired. Correct the seasoning with salt and
pepper. If the sauce is for feathered game and hence no marinade is
available, finish the sauce with a teaspoon of lemon juice. Used for
furred or feathered game that has been roasted or sautéed.

SAUCE au SANG

1 glass (4 ounces)　　　　2 chopped shallots
　red wine　　　　　　　2 tablespoons Brown Sauce
5 crushed peppercorns　　　(or thick gravy)
1 small bay leaf　　　　　Blood and juice from crushed
½ teaspoon thyme　　　　　duck carcass

Put wine, peppercorns, bay leaf, thyme and shallots in a saucepan.
Bring to a boil and cook until reduced to one third the original
quantity. Add Brown Sauce and rub through a fine sieve. As soon
as duck is cooked (and this sauce is only for very underdone duck)
and the breasts have been removed for serving, put legs, bones
and all the carcass in a duck press and press out all the blood and
juice possible. Add this slowly and carefully to the sauce, stirring
it near but not over the fire until the sauce thickens. Do not let
boil after adding the blood. If no Brown Sauce or gravy is available
add Manie Butter, made by creaming 1 tablespoon butter with
½ teaspoon flour, to the reduced wine mixture. When well blended,
add the blood and juice from the pressed carcass and strain through
a fine sieve. Used for wild duck roasted underdone.

QUICK SAUCE for FURRED GAME

2 tablespoons butter
2 teaspoons finely chopped
    shallots (or onion)
2 teaspoons flour

⅔ cup red wine
⅓ cup liquor from uncooked marinade
2 teaspoons red currant jelly
Salt and pepper

Remove game from pan in which it was cooked and pour off all the fat from the pan. Add butter, shallots and flour. Mix all together and cook about 2 minutes. Add wine and blend with mixture in pan, then add marinade liquor, stirring it in slowly and cooking all together about 10 minutes or until the sauce thickens. Add currant jelly, correct seasoning with salt and pepper and pour over game. Used for furred game that has been marinated in an uncooked marinade and then roasted or sautéed.

ROSEMARY (ROMARIN) SAUCE

½ cup red wine
1 teaspoon dry rosemary

2 cups boiling Grand Veneur
    Sauce (page 126)

Bring wine to a boil, add rosemary and let stand for a few minutes to make an infusion. Strain into the Grand' Veneur Sauce. Used for large furred game, especially for that with a heavy game flavour like boar.

ROUENNAISE SAUCE Number II

1 glass (4 ounces) red wine
5 peppercorns
1 small bay leaf
½ teaspoon thyme
2 chopped shallots

2 tablespoons Brown Sauce
    (page 68)
2 or 3 finely chopped duck or
    chicken livers
1 pony (2 ounces) cognac

Put wine, peppercorns, bay leaf, thyme and shallots in a saucepan. Bring to a boil and cook until reduced to one third the original quantity. Add Brown Sauce, return to the boil and remove from heat putting it where it will keep warm. Add livers, mix all together and rub through a sieve. If any of the blood of the duck is available, stir this slowly into the sauce. Add cognac. Used for wild or domestic duck. See also Rouennaise Sauce, Number I, page 80.

VENISON SAUCE

Bring to a boil 2 cups Poivrade Sauce (page 122) and add 2 tablespoons red currant jelly. When jelly is melted, strain through a fine sieve. Used for large furred game.

SUEDOISE SAUCE
(Cream Sauce for Wild Birds)

Remove bird from roasting pan, holding it up to let the juice from its inside drip into the pan. Discard the fat from the pan by skimming it very carefully from the surface of the juice. Then follow recipe for Cream Sauce for Venison (page 124) making it in the roasting pan with the juice of the bird in it and omitting the Poivrade Sauce. Used for all wild birds.

The following recipes are examples of dishes
sauced the French Way with Game Sauces.

GRENADIN of VENISON ST. HUBERT

Cut slices from the loin of venison, having them about 1½ inches thick. (They will look like filet mignon.) Cover with raw marinade and store in the refrigerator for 2 days or longer. When ready to cook them, remove from the marinade and drain well, then dry thoroughly with a towel. Cover the bottom of a frying pan with salad oil and heat very hot. Put in the slices of venison and cook about 3 to 4 minutes on each side. If there are several slices to be cooked use two pans because putting too much meat in a pan will cool the oil and the meat will have a stewed look and flavour instead of the browned, sautéed result. Serve with Poivrade or Cream Sauce.

CHICKEN en CIVET

2½ to 4 pound chicken
¼ cup diced fat salt pork
   (or bacon)
2 tablespoons butter
½ teaspoon salt
A little pepper
12 small onions
12 small mushrooms
1 teaspoon chopped shallots

1 clove garlic, crushed
2 tablespoons flour
1 pint red wine
Faggot made by tying together
   3 sprigs parsley, 1 stalk
   celery, 1 bay leaf and a
   little thyme
Chopped parsley
Blood of chicken (if available)

If chicken is freshly killed and blood can be saved, mix it with a little vinegar (to prevent curdling) and use in sauce.

Clean and singe chicken and cut in 8 pieces (legs and second joints, wings, breasts and back). Season pieces with salt and pepper. Parboil pork dice (or bacon) in water to cover for 5 minutes and drain. Put butter in saucepan, add pork dice and cook until golden brown. Remove dice from fat and reserve. Put chicken in the hot fat and cook until golden brown on all sides. Add onions and mushrooms, cover pan and continue cooking over low heat until onions are a little soft and are starting to brown. Pour off half the fat from the pan, add shallots and garlic to pan and sprinkle in the flour. Cook a few minutes over low heat, stirring to prevent scorching (or put pan in hot oven) to brown flour. Add wine (liquid should just cover chicken, if not enough add a little water or more wine), add faggot, bring to a boil, add pork dice, cover

pan and cook in a moderately hot oven or simmer gently on top
of range about 35 to 40 minutes or until chicken is tender. Skim
fat from surface, remove faggot and correct seasoning with salt and
pepper. If blood has been saved add a little sauce from the pan to it,
then return this to the pan, turn off heat and combine by moving
pan in a circular motion. Never let sauce boil after adding blood.
Put chicken in a hot serving dish, with onions and mushrooms on
top, pour sauce over and sprinkle with parsley. Serve boiled potatoes separately. Serves four or five.

CIVET of VENISON

3 pound venison (shoulder, neck
or other less tender parts)
⅓ cup salad oil
1 cup diced fat salt pork
12 to 15 small onions
½ pound mushrooms
2 tablespoons flour

1 clove garlic, crushed
1 glass red wine
1 faggot (2 stalks celery, 4
sprigs parsley, ½ bay leaf,
pinch of thyme tied to-
gether with string)
Chopped parsley

Remove skin, tough sinews and bones from the meat and cut in
pieces for stew. Cover with raw marinade and put in refrigerator
overnight or longer. When ready to prepare civet, remove meat
from marinade, drain well and dry each piece thoroughly with a
towel. Put oil in frying pan and when hot add the pork dice. Cook
until golden brown, remove them and set aside to add later. Add
onions to same fat and when they have started to brown add carrots, sprinkle with a little sugar and continue cooking until all
are brown, about 5 minutes. Remove them and set aside with the
salt-pork dice. Add the mushrooms, which have been cleaned and
large ones cut in quarters, and sauté them in the fat until they
are soft and the moisture is cooked out of them. Add to the pork
dice and vegetables. Cook the well-dried pieces of meat in the
fat until brown all over, taking care not to crowd the pan. Cooking
a few pieces at a time will insure browning. Remove from fat,
put in saucepan and sprinkle the flour over the meat. Cook until

the flour is brown. Add wine, faggot, garlic, the strained marinade liquor and enough water to cover the meat. Bring to a boil and simmer 1 hour. Add onions, carrots, mushrooms and pork dice and cook 40 minutes longer or until meat is tender. Remove faggot and season to taste. Serve sprinkled with parsley. Serves eight.

ROAST QUAIL

Clean the quail, wrap them in grape leaves and then in slices of fat salt pork. Tie securely with string. Place in roasting pan, spread with a little butter, and put in a very hot oven of 450 to 475 degrees F. Cook 12 to 15 minutes, basting frequently. After removing from pan, make gravy by adding a little water, cooking and stirring in all the browned juice in the pan. If desired add 1 tablespoon dry Sherry and ¼ cup white seedless grapes to gravy in pan for each quail cooked. Serve each bird on toast spread with Rouennaise or liver paste. Serve with wild rice (if obtainable) or Risotto with chopped ham. One bird serves one person.

PHEASANT, SMITANE SAUCE

Clean pheasant and truss to hold legs and wings close to the body. Cover breast with slices of fat salt pork or bacon, tying it on with a string. Season with salt. Place on its side in roasting pan or casserole and spread with good fat. Put in a hot oven of 450 degrees and roast, basting frequently, about 15 minutes. Turn on to other side and cook 15 minutes longer. Turn it on its back and decrease heat to 400 to 425 degrees and cook 10 to 15 minutes or until done, basting all the time. To test if done, lift bird and let juice run out. If the juice which comes out is clean with no pink tinge, the bird is done. Remove to serving dish. Pour off the fat from the pan. Add 2 tablespoons of butter, 1 teaspoon of chopped shallots, 2 tablespoons of vinegar and let reduce to almost nothing. Add 1 cup of cream and cook stirring in all the crustiness around the pan and on the bottom, until reduced to one half the original amount. Thicken with 3 tablespoons of Cream Sauce (page 40) (or Velouté, page 41). Correct seasoning with salt and a little freshly ground white pepper. If sharper sauce is desired, add a few drops of lemon juice. Strain the sauce through a fine sieve and pour over the carved bird or serve the sauce separately.

SALMIS of PHEASANT (or other Game Bird)

Clean and roast the pheasant (above). Remove breasts and legs. Put breasts on warm plate and spread with butter or fat from roasting pan to keep the meat from drying out, cover and put where it will keep warm. Prepare the sauce as follows:

2 tablespoons salad oil
1 chopped onion
1 chopped shallot (if available)
1 clove garlic, crushed
1½ tablespoons flour
1 glass (⅝ cup) red or white wine
1 cup stock (or canned tomatoes)

3 peppercorns
1 faggot (2 stalks celery, 4 sprigs parsley, ½ bay leaf, a little thyme tied with a string)
Legs of roast pheasant
Chopped carcass (bones, skin, etc.) of roast pheasant
12 cooked mushrooms

Heat oil in bottom of saucepan, add onion and cook until onion starts to turn golden. Add shallot, garlic and flour and cook a few minutes. Add wine and cook stirring constantly until thick. Add stock (or tomatoes), salt, peppercorns, faggot, and the legs and chopped carcass of the pheasant. Simmer 1 hour. Remove legs, take off and discard skin. Cut meat from bone and cut in 3 or 4 slices. Cut the reserved breasts, each breast into 3 or 4 slices. Put sliced breast and leg meat in serving dish, place cooked mushrooms on top. Season the sauce to taste and strain over meat and mushrooms. Garnish with toast spread with Rouennaise or any liver paste.

VII. DESSERT SAUCES

VII. DESSERT SAUCES

CATERING for American appetites requires an agile hand with *les entremets riches et délicieux*, and with the sauces that are the final flourish for these dessert masterpieces. Whereas a French woman looks to her *Coq au Vin* or *Blanquette de Veau* for culinary laurels, her American cousin is more apt to seek them with a frozen dessert, sweetly sauced and lavish with whipped cream. In France only a special occasion – wedding, christening, feast day or other party – warrants an elaborate dessert. And then the skill of the local *pâtisserie* – pastry shop – usually produces it.

Every city and most small towns, particularly if the neighbourhood boasts fine chateaux, has its excellent *pâtisserie*. My apprenticeship, like that of so many chefs trained in France, was served in one of these *pâtisseries*, mine in the Maison Calondre in Moulins. Moulins lay in the heart of a lovely countryside where many of the old French aristocracy maintained beautiful chateaux, a retired nobility devoted to fine living. A very exacting clientele. Their cooks, even those in the best-staffed chateaux, were never expected to prepare the fancy desserts served at dinner parties, soirées and other functions. The Maison Calondre made and delivered them and a *chef apprenti* went along to unmould, sauce and garnish the foods he had already helped to prepare. This training in making and serving the most elegant of confections was of untold value to me when many years later I directed the cuisine that catered to American gourmets.

Making the sweet French sauces is fundamentally not much different from making the entrée sauces. That is, you learn how to make the basic ones and then you can prepare almost all the others by combining or varying the basic formulas.

First in the category of sweet sauces comes the custard type, which is called in French either *Sauce Vanille* or *Crème à l'Anglaise*, in English either Vanilla Sauce or Custard Sauce. This is the foundation for more other sauces than any other basic sweet sauce. It is often served plain or flavoured with chocolate, coffee, or other flavour on lady fingers or macaroons. Or topped with an egg-white-and-sugar meringue it becomes one of the most popular of French desserts, the well-known *Oeufs a la Neige* (called Floating Island in this country). This in turn is varied by the addition of berries or sliced fruit. French *Sauce Vanille* is, however, usually richer than American soft custard and the French prefer to flavour their sauce with vanilla bean instead of the extract. They are very careful in making it, too, mixing and stirring with a wire whip constantly during cooking and finally straining it through a fine sieve and so produce a sauce that is lightly delicate and velvety smooth. *Sauce Vanille* or Vanilla Sauce and its many variations are used with Soufflés, *Bavaroises* (Bavarian Creams), *Beignets Soufflés* (a light type of fritter) and also with fruit, usually fresh fruit in season.

For desserts made with various starches such as Rice Puddings, *Beignets* (fritters), Cabinet Pudding and also for cooked fruit, fruit sauces are often preferred to the custard-type sauces. There are two kinds, sweetened fruit purées and sweetened fruit juices that are thickened with arrowroot or cornflour. The most important of these fruit sauces is Apricot Sauce, which is used in several ways in saucing desserts and in coating them, especially if they are to be *flambéed* with liqueur that is ignited and brought to the table flaming. The Apricot Sauce can be made either with apricot jam or with dried apricots.

The following pointers should prove helpful in perfecting your skill in making Dessert Sauces.

... *Sauce Vanille* like any custard mixture curdles very easily. Therefore be sure to mix some of the hot milk with the egg-yolk and sugar mixture, then stir all together briskly and continue stirring every minute while the sauce is over the heat. But the minute it thickens, remove from the heat and set the pan in cold water to check further cooking and possible curdling.

... To prevent a thin skin from forming over the top of a sauce while it cools, stir it frequently.

... The Chocolate Sauce made from the *Sauce-Vanille* base is served cold and used with Vanilla Soufflé, *Bavaroise* (Bavarian Cream) and Lady Fingers. The other Chocolate Sauce, made with chocolate, sugar and water is served warm and used with Profit-erolles, Ice Cream, *Pear Hélène* and other desserts for which a warm sauce is preferred.

∴ ... *Sauce Mocha* or Coffee Sauce has a fresher, more delicious flavour if made with coffee beans (as described on page 143) than when made with bottled coffee extract.

... Sabayon Sauce must be cooked very carefully in a double boiler in much the same way that Hollandaise is made and should be about the consistency of a light Hollandaise.

... *Sauce Vanille* can be stored for a few days in a covered jar in the refrigerator. The fruit sauces can be stored for about a week. Apricot Sauce and *Sauce Reine-Claude* will keep longer than a week if a little liquor is poured on the top as a preservative.

... Use Caramel Syrup to coat moulds or dishes in which cus-tards and rice puddings are baked and the dessert will have a beautiful golden brown glaze when unmoulded as well as a delici-ous flavour.

... When using rum or a liqueur in sauces be careful not to overdo it. A little goes a long way and the flavour of a sauce can be ruined if too much is used.

VANILLA SAUCE
or CREME à l'ANGLAISE

1 cup milk	½ cup sugar
1 cup cream	½ teaspoon flour (optional)
½ a vanilla bean	½ cup whipped cream
4 or 5 egg yolks	(optional)

Scald milk and cream with vanilla bean in top of double boiler. Whip egg yolks and sugar together until mixture becomes very light and combine with milk and cream, stirring vigorously with a whip or slotted spoon. Cook over gently boiling water, stirring constantly, until mixture is thick like a custard. It should coat the back of a spoon as it is withdrawn from the mixture. Strain through a fine sieve or cheesecloth. Cool, whipping from time to time to keep it smooth. If a thicker sauce is preferred, add the flour to the sugar and egg yolks. This sauce can be kept for a couple of days in a refrigerator. If a lighter and richer sauce is desired, fold in the whipped cream just before serving it.

CREME CHANTILLY

Add 1 tablespoon sugar and a few seeds scraped from the inside of a vanilla bean to 1 cup whipped cream. Or instead of the vanilla-bean seeds, add ¼ teaspoon vanilla extract. Used for cold puddings, and to decorate cold and frozen desserts.

APRICOT SAUCE Number I

1½ cups apricot jam	2 tablespoons sugar
½ cup water	2 tablespoons kirsch (or other liqueur)

Put apricot jam, water and sugar in a saucepan and bring to a boil. Cook slowly 5 to 10 minutes, stirring frequently to prevent scorching. Rub through a sieve and add liqueur.

APRICOT SAUCE Number II

¼ pound dried apricots   *¼ cup sugar*

Soak apricots in water to cover for several hours. Bring to the boil and simmer until they are soft. Rub through a sieve and add sugar. Return to heat and cook until sugar is dissolved. If too thick add a little water and cook until it is well combined with the mixture.

CARAMEL SYRUP

Mix together equal parts of sugar and water and cook in a heavy shallow pan until the water evaporates and the syrup becomes golden. As soon as it reaches the desired colour, place the pan immediately on ice or set in cold water to stop the cooking and prevent a dark bitter-flavoured syrup. Used to flavour desserts, coat moulds for desserts and to flavour Bavarian Cream and ice cream.

CARAMEL SAUCE

Add a little water to Caramel Syrup (above) and cook until it is combined and reaches the desired thickness. Used for ice cream, Bavarian Cream and puddings.

CARDINAL SAUCE

1 cup raspberry pulp   *1 cup sugar*
1 cup strawberry pulp   *2 teaspoons cornflour*

Put raspberry and strawberry pulp in a saucepan and bring to the boil. Skim well. Mix sugar and cornflour and add to pulp. Continue cooking until sauce is thick. Rub through a fine sieve. Used for fruit.

CHOCOLATE SAUCE Number I

*3 to 4 ounces sweet chocolate (or
2 ounces bitter chocolate and
2 tablespoons sugar)*

*3 tablespoons hot water
2 cups Vanilla Sauce
(page 140)*

Dissolve chocolate (or chocolate and sugar) in hot water. Mix well and add slowly to Vanilla Sauce. Serve cold. Used for soufflés, Bavarian Cream and desserts made with lady fingers.

CHOCOLATE SAUCE Number II

2 cups water   1 pound grated sweet cooking chocolate

Put water and chocolate in a saucepan, bring to the boil and cook until smooth. Rub through a fine sieve. Serve warm. Used for ice cream, Profiterolles, *Pear Hélène* and puddings.

CREPE SUZETTE BUTTER

*½ cup sweet butter
2½ tablespoons sugar
Grated rind 1 orange
Juice of 1 orange*

*Juice of ½ lemon
1 pony (1 to 2 ounces)
    Curaçao or Cointreau
1 pony (1 to 2 ounces) brandy*

Cream butter, add sugar and orange rind and mix all together well. Add orange and lemon juice and mix well. Add the liqueurs. To use, pour over the crêpes, sprinkle with sugar and brandy and *flambé* – or ignite. This sauce can be made in advance and stored in the refrigerator. When ready to use, cream together all the ingredients.

MOCHA SAUCE

3 tablespoons roasted coffee beans
1 cup hot milk
1 cup of hot cream
4 to 5 egg yolks

¼ cup sugar
1 teaspoon flour (optional)
¼ cup whipped cream
(optional)

Put coffee beans in a pan and place in a hot oven for 3 to 4 minutes – just long enough to heat them through and release the flavour. While hot crush them coarsely and add to the milk and cream. Bring to the boil and strain. Beat egg yolks with sugar until light, combine with the hot milk and cream stirring vigorously with a whip. Cook over boiling water, stirring constantly until the mixture is thick like a custard. (The sauce should coat the back of the spoon as it is withdrawn from the pan.) Strain through a fine sieve or cheesecloth. If a thicker sauce is desired, mix the flour with the egg yolks before combining them with the milk and cream. If a richer sauce is desired, fold in the whipped cream to the chilled sauce just before serving it. Served cold. Used for soufflés and other desserts or served with lady fingers.

RUM-FLAVOURED MOCHA SAUCE

Add 2 tablespoons rum to Mocha Sauce and when cold fold in ¼ cup whipped cream. Used for soufflés and other desserts or served with lady fingers.

FRUIT SAUCE

1 cup fruit juice (cherry, plum, strawberry, raspberry or apricot, etc)
¼ cup sugar (if juice is unsweetened)

Juice of ½ lemon
1 teaspoon arrowroot (or cornflour)
2 more tablespoons of the cold fruit juice

Combine fruit juice, sugar (if unsweetened juice is used) and lemon juice in a saucepan and bring to the boil. Mix arrowroot (or cornflour) with remaining cold fruit juice and add to boiling juice. Cook until clear and slightly thickened. Serve hot or cold. Used for fruit, ice cream and other desserts.

HARD SAUCE

⅓ cup sweet butter
½ cup icing sugar

Few drops vanilla or other flavouring

Cream butter until very soft. Gradually add sugar and flavour with vanilla or other flavouring. Used for hot puddings, especially steamed puddings.

JUBILEE SAUCE

1 cup juice from Black Bing Cherries
1 teaspoon arrowroot (or cornflour)

2 more tablespoons cold fruit juice
1 pony (2 ounces) cognac or kirsch

Cook cherry juice until reduced to ⅔ cup. Mix arrowroot (or cornflour) with the 2 tablespoons of cold juice and add to the hot cherry juice. Continue cooking until clear and slightly thickened. Heat the drained cherries and pour the hot sauce over them. Sprinkle the cognac (or kirsch) on top and ignite. Used for cherries and with ice cream.

RASPBERRY SAUCE

⅓ cup raspberry juice
½ cup melted currant jelly

1 teaspoon arrowroot or cornflour
2 tablespoons cold raspberry juice

Put the ½ cup raspberry juice and currant jelly in a saucepan and bring to the boil. Mix arrowroot (or cornflour) with the cold raspberry juice and add to boiling liquid. Cook until clear and slightly thickened. Serve cold. Used for fruit and other desserts and ice cream.

STRAWBERRY SAUCE

Follow recipe for Raspberry Sauce (above) substituting strawberry juice for raspberry juice.

RED CURRANT SAUCE

Cook red currant jelly until completely melted. Or mix 1½ cups red currant juice with 1½ cups sugar and boil 15 to 20 minutes or until thick. If using a sugar thermometer cook to 238 degrees F. Used for fruit.

RICH SAUCE

½ cup Vanilla Sauce (page 140)   1 pony (2 ounces) liqueur (Grand
1 cup whipped cream   Marnier, Cointreau, Prunelle, etc)

Mix Vanilla Sauce with liqueur and fold in whipped cream. Used for soufflés, Bavarian Cream and other puddings.

PARISIENNE SAUCE

½ cup Vanilla Sauce   1 pony (2 ounces) Maraschino
  (page 140)   liqueur
½ cup puréed fresh strawberries 1½ cups whipped cream
  (wild berries preferred)   1 drop pink vegetable colour

Mix Vanilla Sauce with strawberries and add Maraschino liqueur. Fold in whipped cream and add vegetable colour. Used for berries and other fruits.

RUM SAUCE

Follow recipe for Rich Sauce (above) using rum instead of liqueur. Used for soufflés, Bavarian Cream and baked custard.

SAUCE REINE-CLAUDE Number I

Follow recipe for Apricot Sauce Number I (page 140) using greengage jam instead of Apricot jam.

SAUCE REINE-CLAUDE Number II

1 pound fresh greengages	*⅛ cup water*
¾ pound sugar	*1 pony (2 ounces) kirsch*

Cut and remove stones from greengages but do not peel them. Cook sugar and water together until it spins a thread (238 degrees F. if a sugar thermometer is used). Add greengages to the syrup and cook about ½ hour or until they are soft and the mixture is thick. Rub through a sieve and add kirsch. Used for fruits and puddings.

SABAYON SAUCE

4 egg yolks	*1 cup white wine (or Marsala)*
⅛ cup sugar	*1 tablespoon rum (or kirsch)*

Whip egg yolks and sugar together until mixture becomes very light and lemon coloured. Stir in wine (or Marsala) and put in the top of a double boiler with cold water in the bottom. Cook, stirring constantly, until the water in the bottom comes to the boil or until the mixture become creamy and thickened. Add rum (or kirsch). Serve hot. Used for pudding soufflé, English plum pudding or other warm pudding.

SAUCE à la RITZ

Follow recipe for Rich Sauce (page 145) using Grand Marnier for the liqueur. Used for fruit, soufflés, Bavarian Cream and puddings.

CREAM PATISSIERE

4 egg yolks, beaten	1 teaspoon cornflour
⅛ cup sugar	2 cups scalded milk
6 tablespoons flour	1 vanilla bean (or ⅛ teaspoon extract)

Work up the egg yolks and sugar together until creamy and light. Add flour and cornflour. Gradually add milk in which vanilla bean was scalded. Let cook, stirring constantly, until thick and boiling. Set pan immediately in cold water to cool it quickly or empty into a cold bowl. Stir occasionally to keep a skin from forming on top. Chill before using. May be flavoured with coffee extract to make a mocha cream or with chocolate. Used for filling éclairs, napoleons and other cakes.

CREAM WITH BUTTER

Mix together 1 cup cold Cream Pâtissière with 1 cup butter that has been creamed with 1 tablespoon sugar. Used for filling cakes.

The following recipes are examples of dishes
sauced the French way with Dessert Sauces.

BEIGNETS SOUFFLES

1 cup water (or milk and water)	1 cup flour
½ cup butter	4 eggs
½ teaspoon salt	Flavouring (lemon, vanilla
1 teaspoon sugar	or rum, as desired)

Put water, butter, salt and sugar in saucepan and bring to a boil.
Remove from heat and add flour. Return to fire and cook, stirring
briskly, until mixture rolls away from sides of pan without stick-
ing to them. Add eggs one by one, mixing well after each addition.
Add flavouring. To cook, fill a tablespoon full of the mixture and
slip half of it off into deep hot fat or oil. Then slip off other half
of mixture, making two beignets from each tablespoon. The fat
should be moderately hot at first and gradually made hotter to
brown the beignets. When brown on the underside they will turn
themselves over. When they finish turning over and are golden
brown they are done. Drain well. Put in hot serving dish and
sprinkle with powdered sugar. Serve plain with Vanilla Sauce
(page 140) or Apricot Sauces (pages 140, 141).

CREPES SUZETTE

⅜ cup flour	2 egg yolks
1 tablespoon sugar	1¾ cups milk
Pinch of salt	2 tablespoons melted butter
2 whole eggs	1 teaspoon cognac or rum (optional)

Mix together flour, sugar and salt. Beat eggs and egg yolks together and mix with dry ingredients. Add milk and stir until
smooth. Add butter and liqueur. Strain through a fine sieve. This

batter should be made up about 2 hours before using. To make the crêpes, put a little butter in a very hot frying pan, just enough to grease it. Pour in a very thin layer of crêpe batter. When set and brown on the underside (which takes about a minute), turn on the other side and cook until golden brown. The pan must be very hot because the quicker they cook the better they are. Long cooking toughens them. Fold in quarters and put in hot serving dish with Crêpe Suzette Butter (page 142). Flambé and serve. Makes 12 crêpes.

BERRIES PARISIENNE

Clean berries (strawberries, raspberries, etc), drain and chill. Sprinkle with sugar and a little kirsch or Maraschino liqueur. Serve with Parisienne Sauce (pages 145, 146).

CROUTES aux FRUITS

Cut stale brioche or sweet buns or coffee cake in ½-inch slices, place in baking pan, sprinkle with a little sugar and bake in hot oven of 400 to 425 degrees until golden brown. Prepare a macedoine of fruit – pears, apples, peaches, oranges, pineapple or any desired combination. If possible select fruits of different colours. Boil the fruit in a little sugar syrup and thicken it with enough Apricot Sauce (page 141) for a saucelike consistency. Flavour with rum or kirsch to taste. Make a ring of the browned brioche, bun or coffee-cake slices and fill centre with hot fruit. This is very attractive and delicious if served 'flambé', done by pouring a little hot rum or other liquor on top of the fruit and igniting it at the table just before serving.

PEACH or PEAR CARDINAL

Stewed pears served with Raspberry Sauce (page 144) and sprinkled with shredded almonds.

VANILLA SOUFFLE

2 tablespoons butter   1 piece vanilla bean (or a little extract)
1 tablespoon flour   4 to 5 egg yolks
¼ cup scalded   6 egg whites
   milk   ¼ cup sugar

Melt butter, add flour and cook until it starts to turn golden. Add milk and vanilla bean and cook over low heat, stirring constantly, until it thickens and then continue cooking, stirring occasionally, 3 to 5 minutes. Beat egg yolks and 3 tablespoons sugar together and combine with the milk mixture. Remove vanilla bean (or add extract). Beat egg whites stiff, adding remaining tablespoon sugar during last few minutes of beating. Fold carefully into the mixture, cutting through the mixture, raising and folding it over and over until the whites are completely but lightly incorporated. Pour in a buttered and sugared baking dish and bake in a hot oven of 425 degrees 18 to 20 minutes. Serve immediately with Rich Sauce (page 145). Serves three to four.

INDEX